"Dr. Jesse L. Nelson's *Preaching Life-Chan*ging rich chapters that will help any preacher—lay or trained—in the preaching of God's Word. Dr. Nelson carefully instructs his readers to pray, to select a text, to study the text thoroughly, to structure the sermon carefully, to speak with the power of the Spirit, and to share the gospel with grace. The various examples provided and encouragement gained from reading and practicing the wisdom found in these pages will set any preacher on a path to preaching power."

—Scott M. Gibson, DPhil,
Director, PhD Program in Preaching,
Truett Seminary, Baylor University

"Dr. Jesse Nelson is the real deal. His experience in the pulpit, passion for preaching, keen theological insight, and practical tools for communicators make this book a treasure. *Preaching Life-Changing Sermons* brings God's Word alive in the heart of the preacher and the worshiper!"

—Rev. Margot Starbuck,
speaker, editor, and author of *Small Things with Great Love*

"Why do preachers spend countless hours preparing individual sermons and sermon series? Surely, they must have a clear target in mind! Not necessarily, argues Jesse Nelson in *Preaching Life-Changing Sermons*. This book reminds us that preachers are called to a holy task of proclaiming a biblical message that evokes transformational discipleship in our listeners through the power of the Holy Spirit. Having known him personally, Nelson not only aspires to preach life-changing sermons, but he also models it with his life."

—Matthew D. Kim,
George F. Bennett Professor of Preaching and Practical Theology,
Gordon-Conwell Theological Seminary;
author of *Preaching with Cultural Intelligence* and *Preaching to People in Pain*

"In a simple, practical, easy-to-understand writing style, Jesse L. Nelson fulfills his promise to the readers of his new book: *Preaching Life-Changing Sermons, Six Steps to Developing and Delivering Biblical Messages*. This book certainly blessed me, and I also appreciated the Foreword by Dr. Robert S. Smith. Nelson's book teaches preachers how to develop and deliver biblical messages in any cultural context, giving good information and wise instruction to preachers with or without a seminary education. I highly recommend this new book for all those who write, teach, and deliver life-changing biblical sermons."

—Denise George,
author of *Called to Forgive: The Charleston Church Shooting,
a Victim's Husband, and the Path to Healing and Peace*

"Jesse Nelson's book, *Preaching Life-Changing Sermons*, gives a homiletical recipe to help serious biblical preachers prepare a solid meal to feed God's people. His recipe consists of total dependency on the Holy Spirit, solid biblical content, practical and creative delivery, and cultural intelligence into the African American preaching tradition. Biblical preachers everywhere need not only read this book but, more importantly, put this recipe into practice."

—Dante D. Wright I, PhD, DMin,
Associate Professor of Christian Studies,
Clamp Divinity School of Anderson University

"It's been rightly said that preachers can't get up and say 'Thus saith the Lord!' until they first know what the Lord saith. My brother and co-laborer, Jesse Nelson, reminds us that transformational preaching begins with the diligent study and right interpretation of the supernatural, inspired text of Scripture. But he doesn't stop there. In *Preaching Life-Changing Sermons*, he goes on to equip us with the best practices of expository sermon-making and delivery, all served up with the flavor and fervor of the rich African American preaching tradition, to which all preachers are deeply indebted and from which we have much to learn. Glean from this book the simple profundity of saying what God says with anointing, conviction, authority, and passion. And then use it to train others on your watch to do the same."

—Jim Shaddix, PhD, DMin,
W. A. Criswell Professor of Expository Preaching,
Senior Fellow, Center for Preaching and Pastoral Leadership,
Southeastern Baptist Theological Seminary

"An effective sermon is not intended for entertainment or even instruction; it is intended to produce change in the life of the hearer—and the preacher! Jesse Nelson's book *Preaching Life-Changing Sermons* brings both pastoral experience and scholarly insight to the process of sermon preparation, from the illumination of the preacher to the delivery of the message. The book will be valuable to the novice preacher and a refreshing reminder to the pulpit veteran."

—Michael Duduit,
Executive Editor, *Preaching;*
Dean, Clamp Divinity School of Anderson University

"If there was ever a time we needed a book that would affect lives, it is now. Our communities and our families are in turmoil. From political divide, the pandemic, racial tension, and crime that is out of control, many are looking for answers. I believe the answer will not be found in politics, but from the pulpits! This is why Pastor Jesse Nelson's book, *Preaching Life-Changing Sermons,* is so timely! If preachers would apply and put into practice the principles of this book, I have no doubt we would see noticeable change. I pray that we all would see what could happen in our society when we start *Preaching Life-Changing Sermons!*"

—Fred Luter, Jr.,
Senior Pastor, Franklin Avenue Baptist Church, New Orleans;
Former President, Southern Baptist Convention

"Jesse Nelson's pastoral approach to expository, whole-book preaching offers a practical guide to moving our hearers toward being conformed to the image of Christ with every sermon. Filled with contemporary examples of faithful expositors, Nelson simplifies the process of listening to the biblical text for hearing words that give life. The workman who learns from this book will not be ashamed when standing to preach."

—Eric C. Redmond,
Professor of Bible, Moody Bible Institute

PREACHING LIFE-CHANGING SERMONS

Six Steps to Developing and Delivering Biblical Messages

JESSE L. NELSON

KREGEL MINISTRY

Dedicated to
my pastors, Dr. James A. Smith and Rev. James Bland Smith;
my former dean and professor, Dr. Jerry Barlow;
my mother, Martha Ann Nelson;
all the preachers and people that have influenced my preaching;
and all the preachers I have influenced in the past,
am influencing in the present,
and will influence in the future.

"There are three types of sermons.
The one in your hands, the one in your head, and the one in your heart.
When you preach for me, preach the one in your heart."
—Dr. James A. Smith

"Preaching is giving the Bible a contemporary voice under the guidance
and empowering of the Holy Spirit."
—Dr. Jerry Barlow

CONTENTS

FOREWORD

In his inspiring and pragmatic work *Preaching Life-Changing Sermons: Six Steps to Developing and Delivering Biblical Messages*, Jesse L. Nelson approaches his task from the posture of a *hermeneutic of assumption*. He assumes his audience—pastors and preachers with no formal theological training, lay persons, and formally trained practitioners—begin their pulpit work with the understanding that the biblical text undergirds both the development and delivery of the biblical message. In essence, this is a book that implicitly and explicitly stresses the indispensability of a marriage between substance and style, content and contour, development and delivery concerning what to say and how to say it in sermons that are life-changing.

In what is most likely the first homiletical textbook in church history, *De doctrina Christiana*, Augustine divided his treatise into two sections: hermeneutics (the interpretation of the biblical text) and homiletics (the presentation of the biblical text). The section on hermeneutics occupies three of the four books, while the section on homiletics comprises one book. Augustine, a rhetorician himself, stressed hermeneutics over homiletics. To promote life change, the preacher must have something substantive to say while at the same time say it well in order to engage the audience. This book ultimately serves as a bridge that connects textual responsibility to effective delivery. Like a ferryboat, the book takes the reader back and forth between the shores of the biblical text and the contemporary world.

Jesse Nelson is not just a preacher who goes into his sermonic laboratory and emerges from it offering theoretical gems that enrich preaching. Rather, he is both a formally trained pastor/preacher who presents principles and concepts he has tried in the crucible of his pastoral and itinerant ministry. He weighs the concepts and principles in the balance of his listening audience and finds that they are not wanting.

Jesse Nelson has written and released this book to assist preachers on this mighty long journey in order to encourage solid biblical content with effective delivery—the veritable union of revelation and relevance. I highly commend this work to all who desire to preach well!

—Robert Smith Jr.
Charles T. Carter Baptist Chair of Divinity
and Professor of Christian Preaching,
Beeson Divinity School

PREFACE
Five Reasons to Read This Book

Why another preaching book? I am sure this question popped into your mind when you picked up this book. With so many preaching books on the shelf, why should you read this one? I believe you should read this book for the following reasons.

First, this book will fill a cultural gap on your bookshelf, as it includes information on African American preachers—a subject missing in most biblical or expository preaching books. During my final doctoral seminar, I read a chapter on the history of expository preaching as I completed a book review assignment. "What happened to the black expository preachers?" I wondered. I was appalled, upset, and confused. I was appalled because no history of expository preaching written in the twenty-first century should omit black expository preachers. I was upset because I felt my culture was erased from the annals of expository preaching. I was confused because I personally knew the author, and I was aware of the fact that he knew black expository preachers.

Second, this book will expose you to a few nuances of African American expository preaching. This book will not teach you how to preach "black." This book is not written to argue for black preaching. The nuances learned from African American preachers will prepare you to develop and deliver biblical messages in any cultural context.

Third, you should read this book because it simplifies the approach to preparing biblical sermons. This book will teach you six essential skills for developing and delivering biblical messages.

Another reason you should read this book is because you can use this book for group study too. (You can even invite me to lead a preaching workshop in person or online.) Oftentimes, pastors of smaller congregations and associate ministers are not formally trained with skills to preach biblical messages. This book solves that problem. It can be used as a training manual in churches. It can also be a primary or supplementary textbook for Bible college and seminary preaching courses.

Finally, you should read it because this book will help you preach the Word. Some preaching books are more philosophical than pragmatic. This book is designed to be practical, not theoretical. At one time, the ability to attain the skills for developing and delivering life-changing sermons was limited to the preacher who went to seminary. For the minister unable to attend seminary, *Preaching Life-Changing Sermons* brings the seminary classroom to the minister's study.

For the love of preaching,
Jesse L. Nelson

ACKNOWLEDGEMENTS

In everything give thanks; for this is
God's will for you in Christ Jesus.
—1 Thessalonians 5:18

This section has been the most difficult to write because I do not want to overlook anyone who was instrumental in helping me complete this work. From the first words to the last period, many people have assisted me in completing this book. First and foremost, I thank God (the Father, Son, and Holy Spirit) for saving me from my sins and sending me to preach the good news to the poor, prisoners, blind, and oppressed.

Now starts the hard part! I am thankful for the associate ministers of Macedonia Missionary Baptist Church of Panama City, Florida. Their probing questions about how I prepare and preach my sermons initiated the idea to put my expository preaching techniques on paper. Their feedback on the six steps in this book was essential for revising and simplifying the steps. They became better biblical preachers, and I became a better teacher of biblical preaching through our exchange.

Thank you to Denise George and Rebecca Pounds George for discussing this idea with me at the Writer's Retreat at WinShape. Denise George provided me with several resources, ideas, and suggestions, which contributed to the publication of this work. Also, I would be remiss if I did not thank Dr. John Henry Williams Jr. for allowing me to tag along with him to the Writer's Retreat.

Thank you to my professors from New Orleans Baptist Theological Seminary (Dr. Preston Nix and Dr. Dennis Phelps) for providing input on this project prior to me submitting my initial proposal. Their suggestions, critiques, and comments proved helpful.

I want to give a BIG THANK YOU to Margot Starbuck. Her ideas, enthusiasm, and experience helped me create the perfect proposal to submit to WordServe Literary. Margot has a servant's heart and gave me a helping hand when I needed her the most.

Thank you to my literary agent, Keely Boeving of WordServe Literary, for believing in this project and relentlessly pursuing a publisher for it. She promised we would find a home for it, and she did not stop until we did.

Thank you to my comrades of the Evangelical Homiletics Society for the dialogue and reflections regarding the content of this book. Thank you to Dr. Scott Gibson of the Evangelical Homiletics Society for connecting me with Dr. Robert Hand of Kregel. Thank you to Robert and the entire team at Kregel for believing in the value of this project for preaching. The feedback and suggestions from the editorial team were superb. Thank you for making my dream a reality.

I am thankful for my family and friends who provided me with constant encouragement and support as I completed this book. My wife, Catesha, would remind me of deadlines and remained flexible with my shifting schedule to allow me the space and time I needed to complete this book. My children, Jacey and Carey, unknowingly inspire me to strive for greatness. Their excitement for my accomplishments challenges me to pursue the impossible. My father, Jessie Lee Woods Jr., challenged me in my early years of ministry to become a better communicator through my writing and preaching, which is the foundation of this book. I am thankful for my mother, Martha Ann Nelson; though she is in heaven, her spirit encouraged me to finish what I started. My adopted mother, Dorothy Lashay Fleming Smith, shared words of wisdom on how to balance my time with family, ministry, and writing. She even gave me suggestions on how to write my acknowledgements.

Thank you to my friends, Will Watson Daniels (now deceased) and Leroy McLeroy, for stirring up the gift God has given me to preach the Holy Script. Thank you to Tony Carvalho. He allowed my family to live with him for nine months after we became homeless due to Hurricane Michael destroying our residence in October 2018. It was in his home that I wrote and submitted my first proposal for this book. Although it was initially rejected, I was able to rewrite it (several times over with Margot Starbuck) without worrying about where my family would sleep because he provided us with a roof over our heads.

I am thankful for the churches that allowed me to minister to them through the preached word and discover my "preaching voice" during my first fifteen years of ministry. Thank you First African Baptist Church (Eufaula, AL), Saint Peter Missionary Baptist Church (Abbeville, AL), Dothan Community Church (Dothan, AL), and New Vision Church (Dothan, AL).

I am thankful for Macedonia Missionary Baptist Church of Panama City, Florida, where I serve as senior pastor. I thank God for the spiritual and financial support of Macedonia, which enabled me to begin and finish this book. Thank you for providing me the opportunity to employ and sharpen these six steps every week for the past seven-plus years.

I am thankful to the men who adopted me as their spiritual son, Dr. John Henry Williams Jr. (Selma University) and Dr. Robert Smith Jr. (Beeson Divinity School). Thank you John Henry for being a mentor, friend, brother, confidante, and father in the ministry since my senior year in college at Selma University. Your conversations and contribution on application in biblical preaching are invaluable. Thank you "Papa" Smith for guiding my steps in life and ministry by allowing me to walk in your footsteps. As a "grandmaster" of biblical preaching, your feedback on my research was insightful and affirming.

I am thankful to pastors Fred Luter Jr. and A. Louis Patterson Jr. for demonstrating how to creatively, exegetically, and passionately preach biblical messages. Pastor Luter's friendship and brotherhood is enduring. His wisdom empowered me to do more than I believed I was capable of doing as I pastored my church after a natural disaster and began drafting the first chapter of this book. Pastor A. Louis Patterson Jr. inspired me to preach expository sermons when I heard him preach from Genesis 3 at the R. T. Pollard Retreat at Selma University, my alma mater. Also thank you to Dr. E. K. Bailey, Dr. Ralph West, Dr. Maurice Watson, Dr. Lance Watson, Pastor H. B. Charles and many other black preachers who are models of expository preaching in a black-church context that have influenced my style of biblical preaching.

I am thankful for the Jesse Nelson Ministry team. Their proofreading and feedback for this book is priceless. Thank you to the contributors in this book who offered insights from their personal experience of preparing and preaching life-changing sermons.

Finally, thank you (the reader) for reading this book and applying its principles in an effort to impact the lives of your audience through preaching life-changing sermons.

Soli Deo Gloria,
Jesse L. Nelson
February 7, 2021

INTRODUCTION
Preach the Text!

I t's Sunday morning, and you are standing in the pulpit before a waiting congregation. You are a little nervous but excited to deliver the sermon you prepared. You read the Scripture and announce the title of the sermon. You open your mouth and begin to deliver your message. As you envision this moment, reflect on this question: What is your primary goal when preaching a sermon?

Some of us preach to inform people. Our sermons are loaded with facts and statistics about people and places in the Bible. Some of us want to inspire people. We preach sermons that infuse hope in hearts full of despair. Some of us preach to instruct. We want people to know how to do something like pray, forgive the unforgivable, or live a godly life in an ungodly world. And some of us most likely do not have a primary goal at all; we just preach.

I asked myself this same question about fifteen years ago. After thinking about it for a few days, I discovered my primary goal for preaching: to deliver life-changing sermons. Although I like to think my sermons are a balanced mix of information, inspiration, and instruction, my ultimate purpose is to change lives. I hope people will conform to the image of Christ. I pray people will look, live, and love like Jesus Christ when they hear my sermons. I asked one church member how my sermons had changed her life. She replied with the following statement: "Your sermons help me see who I am in Christ and how much God loves me. Your sermons help with my self-esteem and discovering my purpose in life. Your sermons encourage us to grow and thrive in our relationship with God. You also give tools so we can read the Bible and understand it for ourselves." So how do I preach life-changing sermons? The secret is simple. I preach the text!

Have you ever heard a preacher read a passage of Scripture but preach an unrelated subject? This type of preaching is confusing for the congregation. Confusing preaching is the number-one reason Christians give me when they are searching for a new church to attend. At different times, we've probably all been guilty of preaching confusing sermons. There is a surefire way to avoid this, however; that is to *preach the text.*

Why do some preachers read a text but preach a different subject? I think the primary reason is because they are not trained in preparing sermons that focus on the text. Therefore, they focus on preaching a topic instead of the biblical text. But oftentimes this results in sermons that are scattered, unfocused, and unconnected to the Word of God. Each time I stand before my congregation, I want to preach the text I read with *understanding* and *application.* Tony Evans, Jim Shaddix, Martha Simmons, and Beth Moore are effective communicators because they focus on the biblical text.[1] Preaching the text is the key to preaching a life-changing sermon.

How, you may be asking, can you learn to preach the text? How can you prepare a life-changing sermon? The answer is in your hands. This book will teach you the six steps for developing and delivering a life-changing sermon. If you read this book, you will learn how to seek the Spirit, select your Scripture, study the Scripture, structure your sermon, speak in the Spirit, and share the Savior. Each chapter includes personal illustrations, a profile of a preacher who demonstrates that step, and words of wisdom from a preacher on how to

---

1   See *The Power of Preaching: Crafting a Creative Expository Sermon* by Tony Evans; *Power in the Pulpit: How to Prepare and Deliver Expository Sermons* by Jim Shaddix; and *Doing the Deed: The Mechanics of 21st Century Preaching* by Martha Simmons for their approach to preaching biblical messages.

implement it. As a pastor and scholar with more than twenty years of ministry experience, I am bringing the seminary classroom to your study. If you are ready to change your church and community, this book is for you! Turn the page and take the first step to preaching life-changing sermons.

CHAPTER 1

SEEKING THE SPIRIT

What is the first step for preaching a life-changing sermon? Is it thinking of a great idea? Is it choosing the perfect Scripture? Is it preaching your favorite preacher's most popular sermon?

In fact, it is none of the above. When I was preparing to preach my first sermon, I did not know the first step for preaching a life-changing sermon. I acknowledged my call to preach when I was twelve years old. A couple of years later, my pastor asked me if I was ready to preach. I sincerely and naively said yes. As a fourteen-year-old high school freshman, I was not ready to preach my first sermon, but I had four weeks to get ready. I knew the basic Bible stories from Sunday school, and I knew how to write essays on biblical topics. I had won a few statewide biblical essay contests when I was in middle school. However, I did not know anything about preparing or preaching a sermon. So I began seeking the Spirit of God through prayer. After a week of prayer, the Spirit directed me to my preaching text, Luke 4:18–20. I continued to pray, and the Spirit revealed the outline and points of emphasis for my sermon the next week. After more prayer, I wrote the introduction, body, and conclusion of my sermon. I was ready to preach my first sermon, "The Spirit of the Lord Is upon Me!"

Returning to the initial question, What is the first step for preaching a life-changing sermon? It is *seeking the Spirit*. I began by seeking the Spirit as a young preacher, and after years of seminary training and a doctoral degree in expository preaching, seeking the Spirit is still my first step in sermon preparation.

WHY SHOULD WE SEEK THE SPIRIT FIRST?

There are four primary reasons we should seek the Spirit first when preparing a sermon. First, the Spirit is the author of the Bible. According to 2 Peter 1:20–21, "But know this first of all, that no prophecy of Scripture is a matter of one's own interpretation, for no prophecy was ever made by an act of human will, but men moved by the Holy Spirit spoke from God." The Bible is often called God's Word. This is true, but the Bible is also God's words. The Holy Spirit inspired men to write God's words. So the Bible is not a human book. The Bible is God's book written by humans.

In 1 Corinthians 2:10–11, we notice two additional reasons for seeking the Spirit. The apostle Paul wrote, "For to us God revealed [his thoughts] through the Spirit; for the Spirit searches all things, even the depths of God. For who among men knows the thoughts of a man except the spirit of the man which is in him? Even so the thoughts of God no one knows except the Spirit of God." The second reason we should seek the Spirit is because the Spirit is God and knows the thoughts of God. The Spirit knows exactly what God meant when he said it and men wrote it.

The third reason we seek the Spirit is because he reveals the wisdom of God. This wisdom is called illumination. Church history has yielded different views on illumination. Augustine believed illumination was a "part of the general process of gaining knowledge."[1] Daniel Fuller described illumination as "the process by which the Holy Spirit turns the human will around to accept God's teachings."[2] For John Calvin, the Holy Spirit works in the life of the believer by witnessing to the truth and countering the effects of sin so the meaning of the Bible can become apparent to the believer.[3] I believe illumination is when

---

1   Augustine, *The City of God,* 9.16.
2   Daniel Fuller, "The Holy Spirit's Role in Biblical Interpretation," in *Scripture, Tradition, and Interpretation,* eds. W. Ward Gasque and William Sanford La-Sor (Grand Rapids: Eerdmans, 1978), 189–98.
3   John Calvin, *Institutes of Christian Religion* 1.7, 9.

the Holy Spirit opens a Christian's spiritual eyes so they may see and understand the Word of God.[4]

Illumination and revelation should not be confused. Revelation is the communication of God's truth through his written Word (the Bible). Illumination is the understanding of biblical revelation. Through illumination, the Holy Spirit teaches us all the truth and glorifies Christ. However, abiding sin in our lives can hinder the Spirit's ministry of illumination.[5]

Finally, we should seek the Spirit because he is at work in our preaching. How does the Spirit work in your preaching? The Spirit encourages the preacher to live the Word. The Spirit empowers the preacher to proclaim the Word. The Spirit opens the hearts of those who hear and receive the Word. The Spirit applies the Word of God to the listeners' lives. The Spirit produces lasting fruit in the lives of Spirit-filled believers.[6]

HOW DO WE SEEK THE SPIRIT?

Now we know *why* we should seek the Spirit, but *how* do we seek the Spirit? We seek the Spirit of God through spiritual disciplines. Five common spiritual disciplines are prayer (supplication), study, solitude, service, and submission. While all of these disciplines are necessary to a well-rounded spiritual life, I consider prayer and personal Bible study the most important disciplines for ministers. When I begin discipling a new Christian (or an old one), I encourage them to pray and read Scripture daily. If you are going to preach life-changing sermons, prayer and personal Bible study must be essential and foundational in your life and ministry too! I will focus my discussion on prayer because I believe prayer is the most neglected discipline for preachers.

---

4   I agree with Paul P. Enns on this view of illumination; see his explanation in *The Moody Handbook of Theology* (Chicago: Moody, 1989), 175.

5   Charles Caldwell Ryrie, *A Survey of Bible Doctrine* (Chicago: Moody, 1972), 47.

6   Greg Heisler, *Spirit-Led Preaching: The Holy Spirit's Role in Sermon Preparation and Delivery* (Nashville: B&H Academic, 2007), 4.

WHAT IS PRAYER?

What is your definition of prayer? Talking to God? Communication with God? For me prayer is simply *expressing my heartfelt desires to God.* Let me explain. Prayer is *expressing.* This means I am communicating something. I am making something known. I can express my prayers through speaking, thinking, singing, or writing. The Psalms are full of these expressions.

Prayer is *heartfelt.* This means my prayers are genuine. We must pray sincerely and honestly. Jesus said, "And when you are praying, do not use meaningless repetition as the Gentiles do, for they suppose that they will be heard for their many words. So do not be like them; for your Father knows what you need before you ask Him" (Matt. 6:7–8).

Prayer includes my *desires.* Desires are the yearnings and longings of my heart. My desires are twofold. My desires are what I want from God and what God wants for me. Some people tell us not to pray for the desires of our heart; however, God promises to give me the desires of my heart (answer my prayers) if I delight myself in him (Ps. 37:4).

My prayers are directed *to God.* I do not pray to an object. I pray to God. I can pray with boldness and confidence because my prayers are to the Sovereign God. He is the Creator, Sustainer, and Controller of all things. When I pray, I must make known to God the sincere and honest yearning of my heart. In other words, prayer is *expressing my heartfelt desires to God.*

After expressing my heartfelt desires to God, I look and listen for his answer. Over the years I have identified ways God answers my prayers. God responded through His Spirit by bringing a particular thought to mind as I reflect on my issue. He answered my prayer through the Scripture while I am reading and meditating on it. God spoke through sermons that I listened to during the week. Sometimes God used spirit-filled people to provide wise counsel. I have heard answers through Christian songs. I have also seen God speak through special circumstances like an accident or a miraculous blessing.

WHY SHOULD WE PRAY?

Why do you pray? We all pray for various reasons. Some of us pray because we feel obligated. Others of us pray when we feel overwhelmed by our ministry. I pray for several reasons. I pray because Jesus expects his disciples to pray (Matt. 6:5–7). I pray because I cannot receive certain things until I pray (James 4:2). I pray when I want God to reveal the unknown (Jer. 33:3). I pray because I will receive the peace of God (Phil. 4:6–7). I pray because I want to walk in the footsteps of Jesus (Mark 1:35, Luke 6:12). I pray because I want to be filled with the Spirit and speak with boldness (Acts 4:31). I pray because prayer is a weapon for spiritual warfare (Eph. 6:18–20).

WHEN AND WHERE SHOULD WE PRAY?

We should pray at all times! Paul told the Thessalonian Christians to pray without ceasing (1 Thess. 4:17). Praying without ceasing does not mean we should be walking around talking aloud to ourselves all day. Instead, praying without ceasing means we should be walking in the spirit of prayer. This keeps us in constant contact or communion with God. Although you may say "amen" after your morning prayers, you should never stop praying or communicating with God. When you live a life of constant communion with God, you can pray anywhere. You do not have to confine your prayer life to a prayer closet. You can pray in your car, office, break room, or outside because you carry your inner prayer closet with you everywhere you go. We can pray anytime and anywhere.

HOW DO YOU PRAY?

How do you pray? As a child my grandmother taught me to pray the Lord's Prayer. The Lord's Prayer is the model Jesus gave his disciples for praying sincere prayers. Although I have learned various prayer techniques, the Lord's Prayer is still a model for me. I use the acronym PRAY to move through the Lord's Prayer: Praise, Repent, Ask, and Yield.

I start my prayer with praise (Matt. 6:9). I *praise* God for being my heavenly Father. I praise him for my salvation through the death and resurrection of Jesus Christ (the gospel). I praise him for the Holy Spirit who seals and secures me until the day of redemption. I praise God for his compassion, grace, patience, lovingkindness, and truthfulness. I also pray through the names of God and praise him for the characteristics or attributes those names identify. For example, I praise God for being Jehovah Jireh, my provider. I praise God because he is Jehovah Shalom, my peace. I praise God as Jehovah Rapha, my healer and Jehovah Raah, my shepherd.

After praising God, I *repent* of my sins (Matt. 6:12). Sometimes my sins are obvious, so I confess and repent of those first. Sometimes, if the burden of sin is heavy, I confess and repent first in my prayer and then I praise God for forgiveness. When my sins are not so obvious, I think through the Ten Commandments, the Beatitudes, or my daily devotional Scripture and confess the sins where I feel the Spirit's conviction.

Once I finish confessing, I begin to *ask* God for provision and protection for others and myself (Matt. 6:11, 13). When I was a young boy, I was taught the acronym JOY for prayer: Jesus, Others, and Yourself. Based on this principle, I prayed for myself last. But by the time I began praying for myself, I was so exhausted from praying for others that I would basically say "Lord, bless me." However, when studying prayer during seminary, I began reading Dr. John Piper, the retired pastor of Bethlehem Baptist Church in Minneapolis, Minnesota, and the author of many books, including *Desiring God*. In one article I read, Dr. Piper said he prayed in concentric circles.[7] This method has become my primary way of praying for others and myself. How does it work?

In regard to asking for provision and protection, I pray for myself first because if I am not in a good place spiritually, I am no good to anyone else. Then I pray for my household and immediate family by name. Next, I pray for my staff, deacons, and other church leaders by name. I pray for the congregation as a whole—all the members. I also

---

7   "How Do You Structure Your Prayer Life?," interview with Dr. John Piper, DesiringGod.org, November 22, 2017, https://www.desiringgod.org/interviews/how-do-you-structure-your-prayer-life.

pray for pastors, missions, the missionaries we support, and Christians around the world. I pray for leaders of Christian organizations, the community, city, and country. So I begin praying for myself and keep revolving my prayers until I reach the ends of the earth. Finally, you must pray to *yield* or submit your will to God's will (Matt. 6:10). After I finish praying through my circles of needs, concerns, and desires, I say, "Not my will, but your will be done." Although I express my genuine desires to God, ultimately, I want his will to be accomplished in my life because he can do abundantly more than I could ever think or ask of him. I am also asking for his kingdom to come so that we may have a taste of heaven on earth.

HOW DID PREACHERS PRAY IN THE BIBLE?

Let's review the New Testament and see the connection between prayer and ministry. Jesus, a preacher of life-changing sermons, modeled prayer in his life and ministry. Jesus did not stay in bed after a long day of ministry. Jesus got up early the next morning and went to a secluded place to pray (Mark 1:32–35). Jesus prayed all night before choosing his disciples (Luke 6:12–16). Jesus taught his disciples how to pray (Luke 11:1–12). Jesus prayed for his disciples and future generations of Christians (John 17:6–26). Jesus prayed before he was arrested in the garden (Matt. 26:26–46). Jesus prayed while he was being murdered on the cross (Luke 23:34). Jesus is praying for us right now (Rom. 8:34). If Jesus prayed at all times, we should too!

The apostles were men of prayer. Prayer was foundational for their ministry. Jesus taught them how to pray (Luke 11:2–5). Jesus encouraged them to pray at all times (Luke 18). They were praying in an upper room in Jerusalem after the ascension of Christ (Acts 1:14). The apostles prayed when the chief priests and elders released Peter and John from jail (Acts 4:23–31). According to Acts 6, the apostles did not want to neglect the ministry of prayer and the Word. So the apostles appointed seven men to oversee the distribution of food to the widows so that they could remain focused on prayer and the Word. How often have you neglected the ministry of prayer to do something you thought was more important?

Another preacher of life-changing sermons, Paul, also modeled prayer in his ministry. Paul included prayer in every letter he penned to the churches. Paul's prayers serve as a guide for me when praying for my congregation or ministry. Not only am I praying God's Word over my church, I am praying God's Word that was for the church. So if you ever wonder what to pray for your church, Paul's prayers are a perfect place to start.

These men preached life-changing sermons because they were praying preachers. Jesus preached the Sermon on the Mount (Matt. 5–7). Peter preached a sermon, and three thousand people were saved (Acts 2). Paul preached a sermon and people began to believe in the "unknown God" that Paul made known (Acts 17). Since Jesus, the apostles, and Paul were praying preachers, we should be devoted to prayer too.

A PRAYING PREACHER

Dr. Fred Luter Jr. is a life-changing preacher who exemplifies prayer in his preaching. Dr. Luter's ministry began as a street preacher in New Orleans, Louisiana. Within a few years, he became pastor of Franklin Avenue Baptist Church in the Ninth Ward of New Orleans.

Before the devastation of Hurricane Katrina in August 2005, Franklin Avenue Baptist Church was the largest Southern Baptist Church in Louisiana with more than seven thousand members. Since Katrina, his church continues to see more than four thousand worshippers gather on Sunday morning. Pastor Luter, who became the first African-American president of the Southern Baptist Convention in 2012, frequently preaches at Bible conferences, city-wide revivals, and seminary chapel services.

In April of 2015, Dr. Luter was the guest preacher for my church's missions conference. As the host pastor for the conference, I was the head of Dr. Luter's hospitality committee. One day after lunch, I asked Dr. Luter what was the key to his success as a pastor and prolific preacher. Dr. Luter smiled knowingly. "My answer will probably disappoint you," he told me. He went on to explain that the key to his success was his daily devotion with God. He said no matter how busy his pastoral and preaching calendar became, he always took the time to pray and spend time in God's Word each day.

Prayer is the key to Dr. Luter's success. Prayer is how Pastor Luter determines what Scripture to preach. Prayer is what reveals the truth of the text to him. Prayer is what ignites his fiery preaching in the pulpit. Prayer is what opens the people's hearts to receive the gospel of Jesus Christ through him. Each time I hear Dr. Luter preach, he says this prayer before he preaches:

> God, let me decrease as you increase. Father, let them not see Fred, but God, let them see Christ. To the end, God, that you may be glorified, the saints of God may be edified, Satan may be horrified, and all sinners will come to repentance. Therefore God, stand in my body, think with my mind, and speak with my voice. I will be so very careful then to give you all of the praise, all of the glory, and all of the honor. In Jesus's name we pray, and for his sake may the people of God say, "Amen."

How did Dr. Luter go from a street preacher to president of the Southern Baptist Convention? One word: prayer! I am convinced Dr. Fred Luter is a life-changing preacher with a life-changing ministry because he is a praying preacher. As we often say, "I want to be like him when I grow up." So if you want to preach life-changing sermons, you must be a praying preacher!

WORDS OF WISDOM

Charles Haddon Spurgeon was a life-changing preacher who exemplified prayer in his ministry. Spurgeon was a nineteenth-century pastor who preached to thousands each week. It is said Charles Spurgeon took a group of visitors to the boiler room to reveal the power undergirding his preaching ministry. When Spurgeon opened the door, they saw a group of church members praying for Spurgeon. Prayer was the source of his power! In the book *Lectures to My Students*, Spurgeon—sometimes called the "Prince of Preachers"—offers words

of wisdom on prayer and preaching to his students. "Use prayer as
a boring rod, and wells of living water will leap up from the bowels
of the Word. Who will be content to thirst when living waters are
so readily to be obtained! The best and holiest men have ever made
prayer the most important part of pulpit preparation."[8]

Another life-changing preacher named Charles is Dr. W. Charles
Lewis, the founder and senior pastor of Dothan Community Church
in Dothan, Alabama. He is a graduate of Tuskegee University, a historic black college and university in Tuskegee, Alabama. Dr. Lewis
received his master's and doctorate degrees from Dallas Theological
Seminary. He is a professor for the Dothan extension of the Birming-
ham Theological Seminary. He also serves as a church-planting coach,
pastoral mentor, and advocate for racial reconciliation. I served on the
staff of Dothan Community Church as associate pastor of teens for
a couple of years, so I know he practices what he teaches regarding
spiritual preparation. Here are his words of wisdom on seeking the
Spirit:

> The message of God is delivered by the messenger of God,
> and just as the Word of God is unadulterated, the messen-
> ger should be also. Thus, the spiritual preparation of the
> preacher is vital and begins with a spiritual mindset. As a
> messenger of God, he must prepare his sermon with the
> mindset that he has an audience of one to please; that is,
> the triune God (2 Timothy 2:4). Being mindful that he is
> God's messenger (Romans 10:15), the preacher must seek
> to please God in his study of the Word, his living of the
> Word, and his delivery of the Word (Ezra 7:10).
>
> He does not want to be ashamed before his audience (of
> one) so he must be diligent to present himself approved
> to God as a workman who does not need to be ashamed,
> accurately handling the Word of truth (2 Timothy 2:15).

---

8   C. H. Spurgeon, *Lectures to My Students* (Grand Rapids: Zondervan, 1954),
     44.

Therefore, he must objectively study the text in context in order to receive God's message and deliver it without pretext. This is a spiritual undertaking. Secondly, he must be aware of the spiritual nature of his human audience. He must be prepared spiritually in order to minister to them spiritually. This includes prayer, reflection, and meditating on God's Word: "My message and my preaching were not in persuasive words of wisdom, but in demonstration of the Spirit and of power, so that your faith would not rest on the wisdom of men, but on the power of God" (1 Corinthians 2:4–5). Thirdly, he must be a practitioner of the Word that he preaches. His life is to authenticate and validate his message. When the messenger's life matches the message he delivers, it helps to make him a vessel fit for the Master's use: "Therefore, if anyone cleanses himself from these things, he will be a vessel for honor, sanctified, useful to the Master, prepared for every good work" (2 Timothy 2:21).[9]

So, what can we conclude? The first step for preaching a life-changing sermon is seeking the Spirit. I believe the primary, but most neglected way, to seek the Spirit is through prayer. It is never too late to become a praying preacher. Start praying more today . . . right now! After you come back from your time of prayer, turn the page and discover the second step for preaching a life-changing sermon.

---

9   W. Charles Lewis, message to the author, January 27, 2021. Used by permission.

CHAPTER 2

SELECTING THE SCRIPTURE

I t's Saturday night, and Sunday morning is coming. What am I going to preach? I asked this question often when I first started preaching. I always asked the Spirit for guidance on selecting a preaching text. Then I waited for a spiritual hunch or inspiration from some life experience to direct me to a specific Scripture. If I did not receive clarity by Saturday night, I would preach a familiar verse like John 3:16 or a Bible story like Daniel in the lions' den.

Starting and finishing a sermon on Saturday night can be exhausting. My ministry mentor, the late Pastor James Bland Smith, called this a "Saturday night special." And Saturday night specials, Pastor Smith assured me, were not a good thing for preachers. I have prepared a few Saturday night specials during my ministry. How about you? Early in my preaching ministry, I prepared Saturday night specials because I did not have a consistent method for selecting a preaching text.

How do you choose a preaching text? Knowing how to pick a text is essential for preaching a life-changing sermon. If you remember from the last chapter, the first step for preaching life-changing sermons is *seeking the Spirit*. The second step for preaching life-changing sermons is *selecting the Scripture*.

HOW I LEARNED TO SELECT THE SCRIPTURE

When I started my interim pastorate at the age of eighteen, my sermons were "solos." I just preached from week to week, with no connecting thread running between sermons. Sometimes I planned my preaching for about three weeks to a month at a time. However, most of the sermons were not connected to a particular theme. I selected my preaching text one week at a time. My preaching was like pearls without a string, individually beautiful but not forming a whole necklace.

After three years as an interim pastor, I was called to serve in my first pastorate. Ten months later, I began my seminary studies at New Orleans Baptist Theological Seminary. During my second semester, I took "Proclaiming the Bible," a sermon preparation course with Dr. John Thomas. Two of the books I read during the class were *Power in the Pulpit*, by Jerry Vines and Jim Shaddix, and *Seven Steps to the Expository Sermon*, by Ramesh Richard.

Dr. Thomas and the authors of *Power in the Pulpit* recommended selecting a book of the Bible and preaching consecutive sermons through it or portions of it. I tried it, and I liked it. I started preaching through Ephesians 4. Then I moved to the Sermon on the Mount (Matthew 5–7), Malachi, portions of Joshua, and 1 John. Preaching through books of the Bible has been my preferred method for pastoral preaching since I took my first preaching class in seminary.

HOW TO SELECT A TEXT

How do we choose which text to preach? I have learned to ask two "big" questions to help me choose my preaching text. The first is, What does God want to say to the people? I ask this question in prayer and wait to hear from the Lord. I ask this question for several reasons. First, although I think I have a good perspective on life and how people should live, what I have to say to the people is not important. My opinion is not the truth, nor is it always right. However, what God says is always true and right. Second, I am acknowledging the fact that the congregation belongs to the Lord. Therefore, he knows what he wants to say to his people. Usually, he leads me to a topic for a series of sermons or a book to preach through on Sunday mornings. He responds to my question in various ways. I may find my spirit strongly connecting to a Scripture while reading the Bible.

I might be inspired from listening to another sermon. At times I discern the Spirit saying, "Preach this . . .". I may receive a revelation during a time of prayer and meditation. I meditate on three questions:

1. Who does God want the people to be?
2. What does God want the people to do?
3. What does God want the people to know?

Sometimes it may take days or weeks to get an answer. He may only answer one question. For example, he may say that the people need to be joyful. Since Philippians is the letter of joy, I would select my texts from this book. So the first big question is, What does God want to say to the people?

The second big question is, What do the people need to hear from God? I pray through this question too. While praying, I am focusing on five questions:

1. How do the people need to grow in Christ?
2. What sins do the people need to stop? Of course people need to stop all forms of sin, but I am asking which sins are most prevalent in their lives.
3. What doctrine needs to be taught?
4. What spiritual discipline needs to be emphasized, like prayer, evangelism, stewardship, or worship?
5. What Bible book will parallel with the church in this season of ministry and the people's lives?

While waiting on an answer, I am observing the congregation's behavior. I am listening to the biblical, moral, and spiritual questions they ask during Sunday school, Bible study, or small groups. I might ask certain members what they are experiencing in their life, or what questions they have about God or the Bible. Although I observe current events on social media and mass media, I do not allow those media outlets to have a significant influence in my text selection process.

When I became pastor of Macedonia Missionary Baptist Church in 2014, I spent time in prayer and observation asking, What do the people need to hear? After a couple of months, the Spirit led me to preach through Mark and 1 Corinthians. I believe preaching through Mark gave the congregation a solid overview of the ministry of Jesus and his disciples. Preaching through 1 Corinthians addressed numerous topics and issues in the church—for example, the gospel, unity, lawsuits, marriage, divorce, spiritual gifts, and the resurrection of Jesus.

HOW I PREACH THROUGH BOOKS OF THE BIBLE

I preach through books of the Bible in four ways. First, I may preach through the entire book by preaching all of the sections or portions of Scripture in the book. This varies according to the type of Scripture. In the narrative books, I may preach a few verses or an entire chapter, depending on the length of the story. In the letters, I may preach each paragraph or a section of paragraphs related to the same topic. I preached through 1 Corinthians section by section. Some preachers call this systematic or consecutive exposition. Second, I may preach a topic from a book of the Bible. I preached about prayer from the book of Acts. I preached about joy from Philippians. I preached "Who is Jesus?" from John's gospel. Third, I may pick a chapter or section of a certain book and preach through it. For example, I have preached through Psalm 1, Psalm 23, 1 Corinthians 13, Hebrews 11, Ephesians 4, and Philippians 4. Finally, I may preach one passage from each chapter of the book. I preached 1 John and James this way.

FIVE REASONS I PREACH THROUGH BOOKS OF THE BIBLE

Why do I preach through books of the Bible? Some ministers think preaching through a book of the Bible is boring. Although I preach topical sermon series, most of my preaching focuses on preaching through a book of the Bible. Different methods have their merit, but I recommend you preach through books of the Bible for the following five reasons.

First, preaching a series of sermons from a Bible book creates a preaching plan for the minister who preaches on a regular basis. I do not have to wonder what I am preaching the next week; it's whatever comes next in the book. This saves me time and allows me to devote my energy to actually crafting the message and listening for God's input, rather than worrying about what text to select.

Second, preaching a series of sermons from a Bible book will lessen the sermon preparation time. The author, the date of the writing, and the purpose of the book do not change from passage to passage. So when preaching from a book of the Bible for consecutive weeks, I do not have to complete a background study each week.

Third, preaching a series of sermons from a Bible book reveals the unity within that book. The book revolves around a unique purpose. As you preach through a book of the Bible, you reveal that purpose to your congregation as you preach each passage.

Fourth, preaching a series of sermons from a Bible book increases biblical literacy in the congregation. The congregation learns more about a particular book of the Bible and how other Bible passages connect to the text. It takes them deeper into their study because each message will provide depth and breadth in the knowledge of God and his Word.

Fifth, preaching a series of sermons from a Bible book gets you off of your hobbyhorse. The power of prayer is one of my favorite topics to preach. I probably preach on prayer at least once a year, especially during times of corporate prayer and fasting. Some preachers preach the same topics or themes over and over. This limits your church's biblical literacy and spiritual growth. However, preaching through a Bible book exposes the congregation to numerous topics addressed in the Bible. One church member told me, "I like when you preach through books of the Bible because we are learning the whole Word of God."[1]

---

1   Member of Macedonia Missionary Baptist Church, text message to author, April 3, 2019.

A SYSTEMATIC PREACHER

Dr. John MacArthur has served as pastor-teacher of Grace Community Church in Sun Valley, California, since 1969. His weekly attendance exceeds five thousand, and *Preaching Magazine* recognized him as one of the twenty-five most influential pastors in the past twenty-five years.[2] Dr. MacArthur is known for his verse-by-verse method of expository preaching through books of the Bible. John MacArthur took forty-two years to preach through the entire New Testament. His expositional sermons focus on the historical background and grammatical details of the text. In 2015, the MacArthur New Testament Commentary series was completed. These thirty-three volumes are a compilation of Dr. MacArthur's sermons. This commentary series explains every verse of the New Testament.[3]

Why does John MacArthur preach through books of the Bible verse by verse? According to MacArthur, preaching through books of the Bible verse by verse is the best way to teach the whole counsel of God. MacArthur believes this expositional method of systematically preaching through books of the Bible keeps him faithful to fulfill the mandate to teach the whole new covenant (testament). He also thinks preaching through books of the Bible allows the congregation to see the context of each Scripture in relation to the book and the New Testament as a whole. For Dr. MacArthur, it's only logical to preach through books of the Bible verse by verse in order to interpret their meaning in their contexts. Dr. MacArthur said, "If I received five letters in the mail one day, it would make no sense to read a sentence or two out of one, skip two, read a few sentences out of another, and go to the next one and read a few out of that, and on and on. If I really want to comprehend the letter—what is going on, the tone, the

---

2   Michael Duduit, "The 25 Most Influential Pastors of the Past 25 Years," *Preaching Magazine* https://www.preaching.com/articles/the-25-most-influ-ential-pastors-of-the-past-25-years.

3   "About John MacArthur," Grace to You, accessed April 3, 2019, https://www.gty.org/about/john.

spirit, the attitude, and the purpose—I must start from the beginning and go to the end of each one."[4]

WORDS OF WISDOM

Pastor H. B. Charles Jr. also advocates preaching through books of the Bible. Pastor Charles is pastor of Shiloh Metropolitan Baptist Church in Jacksonville, Florida. He is the author of several books, including *On Pastoring* and *On Preaching*. In his book *On Preaching*, he wrote these words of wisdom regarding consecutive exposition (preaching through books of the Bible):

> Consecutive exposition both satisfies people's hunger for Scripture and shapes it. Bible exposition is an acquired taste. Before people experience it, they don't know what they are missing. But once they do, they will not be satisfied with anything else. Consecutive exposition is not the only way to preach faithfully. . . . Yet I contend that consecutive exposition—preaching through a book of the Bible from beginning to end—is the most faithful way to preach.[5]

So the second step for preaching life-changing sermons is selecting the Scripture. I agree with Dr. John MacArthur and Pastor H. B. Charles regarding consecutive exposition. Preach through books of the Bible! I go off-schedule for special days like Christmas, Easter, Mother's Day, and Father's Day. However, the majority of my preaching is through a book of the Bible. Even in the summers I preach through

---

4   "Why Are You Compelled to Preach Verse by Verse through Books of the Bible Unlike Other Notable Preachers Such as C. H. Spurgeon?," interview with Dr. John MacArthur, Grace to You, accessed April 3, 2019, https://www.gty.org/library/questions/QA83/why-are-you-compelled-to-preach-verse-by-verse-through-books-of-the-bible-unlike-other-notable-preachers-such-as-c-h-spurgeon.

5   H. B. Charles, *On Preaching: Personal and Pastoral Insights for the Preparation and Practice of Preaching* (Chicago: Moody, 2014), 58.

Psalms or Proverbs. Start first by preaching through a short book like James, Philippians, Ruth, or Jonah. Then move on to longer books. Try it! You may like it!

CHAPTER 3

STUDYING
THE SCRIPTURE

Who was the first preacher to introduce you to the idea of expository or biblical preaching? For me, two preachers come to mind: Pastor Sanford Johnson and the late Pastor James Bland Smith, my first pastoral mentor. These two men were contemporaries in Eufaula, Alabama in the late 1990s. As a young teenage preacher searching for my preaching voice, I noticed that their preaching style was different than the traditional black preacher in South Alabama. These pastors were "teaching-preachers." They would select a passage of Scripture and preach through it verse by verse. Their sermons included explanations of terms, relevant illustrations, and personal application. These pastors were expository preachers. Actually, the first time I heard the phrase "expository preaching" was when Pastor Smith described Pastor Johnson's preaching style as expository because he preached verse by verse.

Pastor Smith and Pastor Johnson also introduced me to some of my first resources for sermon preparation. Pastor Johnson used the J. Vernon McGee commentaries, and Pastor Smith used the Thompson Chain Study Bible and *Wilmington's Guide to the Bible*. Pastor Smith purchased the Thompson Chain Study Bible for me, which enabled me to both interpret Scripture with Scripture through all the cross-references, and also conduct topical studies. My mom purchased the NIV Study Bible for me. The study notes helped me interpret and apply the text. The book introductions helped me understand the author's purpose, the historical background, and the context of the recipients.

I also became intrigued with expository preaching through the radio ministries of Tony Evans, Chuck Swindoll, Charles Stanley, and David Jeremiah. They always made me wonder how they found those truths in the text. Listening to them made me say, "I want to go to seminary so I can learn how to be an expository preacher."

One of my greatest influences for being a biblical preacher was the late Dr. A. Louis Patterson Jr. Dr. Patterson pastored Mount Corinth Missionary Baptist Church for more than forty years. Many call him a "godfather" of black expository preaching. He influenced thousands of pastors and ministers as the lecturer for the Ministers' Division of the National Baptist Congress of Christian Education of the National Baptist Convention, USA. These lectures and sermons are published in the book *Joy for the Journey: A Collection of Sermons from the Congress of the National Baptist Convention USA Inc.*

I met Dr. Patterson during my first semester at New Orleans Baptist Theological Seminary. Dr. Patterson was the keynote speaker for the R. T. Pollard Retreat at Selma University, my alma mater. Once Dr. Patterson took the microphone, he opened a small black Bible and read from Genesis 3. His sermon captivated me. He was actually preaching the text. He explained words in the text, and his points of emphasis connected to the text. Upon the conclusion of his sermon, I said, "I want to preach like him!" So for the next three years I focused my seminary coursework and extra reading on developing and delivering biblical messages.

After seminary, I learned additional Bible study techniques from Dr. W. Charles Lewis, Senior Pastor of Dothan Community Church in Dothan, Alabama. Dr. Lewis, a graduate of Dallas Theological Seminary, was a student of Howard Hendricks and a friend of Dr. Tony Evans. As associate pastor of teens, I was mentored by Dr. Lewis and studied expository preaching for two years. I have also been influenced by several other preachers: Pastor Fred Luter Jr., Pastor H. B. Charles Jr., Dr. John Henry Williams Jr., Dr. Robert Smith Jr., Dr. Ralph West, Dr. Maurice Watson, Dr. Marcus Davidson, Dr. Lance Watson, and Dr. E. K. Bailey, another pioneer of black expository preaching.

When I think of all the preachers who inspired me to be an expository preacher, the one common denominator between them was their desire to study the Scriptures so they could accurately interpret the Word of God. Although I am different than all of them, I share their conviction. I study the Word so that I can properly interpret it and apply it to my listening audience. Studying the text is the heart of life-changing preaching.

Do you have a zeal for studying Scripture? How do you study the Scripture for sermon preparation? Knowing how to study the Scripture is essential for preaching a life-changing sermon. When we misinterpret the text, our listeners will misapply the text, which can lead to mistakes in their Christian life and missed opportunities in the kingdom of God. Therefore, it is vital that we know how to study the Scripture so we can "rightly divide the Word of truth."

HOW TO STUDY THE SCRIPTURE: FOUR STEPS

Studying the Bible is hard work. In 2 Timothy 2:15, Paul instructed Timothy to study the Word. The word in that verse for "study" can also be translated as "to be diligent." Paul encouraged Timothy to give his best efforts to studying God's Word. Paul wanted Timothy to work hard so he could correctly teach or "rightly divide" the Word of God.

Have you tried to use a butter knife as a screwdriver? I have used a butter knife a few times as a tool. It worked, but it was not the best tool for the job. Sometimes the point of the blade was too thin for the head of the screw. At other times, I could not properly grip the handle. All of this led to my frustration and inability to complete the job appropriately. Just like using a butter knife for a screwdriver, you can mishandle the text by using the wrong tools. You can interpret the text more accurately with the proper techniques and tools. So how do we study Scripture in a way to know we have interpreted it correctly? I will share with you four steps for studying the Scripture.

STEP 1: PRAY

We should ask the Spirit to open our eyes so we can see the truth of the Scriptures (Ps. 119:18). We should also ask the Spirit to guide

us during the process of studying the text. We should thank the Spirit
for the insight and understanding we receive while studying the text.

STEP 2: COMPLETE A HISTORICAL BACKGROUND STUDY

We must understand the text's historical context. This can be accomplished by completing a historical background study. Answering the following ten questions will give you a general overview of the text's historical context:

1. Who is the author of the book?
2. Who are the recipients of the book?
3. When was the book written?
4. Where was the author when he wrote the book?
5. What occasion or events caused the author to write the book?
6. What were the social and cultural norms of the recipients?
7. What was the recipients' understanding of God?
8. What is the purpose of the book? Why was it written?
9. What is the book's literary genre?
10. Where is this book in biblical and world history?

You can use various resources to complete the historical background study.

BASIC RESOURCES FOR A PREACHING LIBRARY

Study Bibles
MacArthur Study Bible (NASB)
The Tony Evans Study Bible

Concordance
Strong's Complete Exhaustive Concordance (NASB)

Dictionary for Words in the Bible
Mounce's Complete Expository Dictionary of Old and New Testament Words

Bible Dictionaries/Encyclopedias
Holman Illustrated Bible Dictionary
New Bible Dictionary

Books on Hermeneutics
Living by the Book—Howard and William Hendricks
How to Read the Bible for All Its Worth—Gordon Fee and Douglas Stuart

Books on Theology
Know What You Believe—Paul E. Little
Christian Theology—Millard J. Erickson
Theology You Can Count On—Tony Evans

Commentaries
The Tony Bible Evans Commentary (1 volume)
New Bible Commentary (1 volume)
Bible Knowledge Commentary (2 volumes—Old and New Testaments)
Expositor's Bible Commentary (12 volumes)
New American Commentary (volumes on individual books of the Bible)
NIV Application Commentary (volumes on individual books of the Bible)
Preaching the Word Commentary Series (volumes on individual books of the Bible)
Tyndale Old and New Testament Commentaries (volumes on individual books of the Bible)

Expository Sermon Books
E. K. Bailey Sermon Series: Volume One—E. K. Bailey and H. B. Charles Jr.
Joy for the Journey: A Collection of Sermons from the Congress of the National Baptist Convention USA Inc.—Pastor A. Louis Patterson Jr.

Software
Logos Bible Software

Online Resources
Thomas Constable Notes on the Sixty-Six Books of the Bible
www.soniclight.org
Bible Gateway
https://www.biblegateway.com/resources
Bible Study Tools
https://www.biblestudytools.com/library

STEP 3: READ THE SCRIPTURE

Life-changing preaching requires that you read, read, and re-read the text you plan to preach. You must internalize the Scriptures. Dr. Robert Smith Jr., professor of Christian preaching at Beeson Divinity School and author of *Doctrine That Dances*, challenges his students to read the text fifty times before they begin to study it.[1] Dr. Jerry Vines, retired pastor and coauthor with Dr. Jim Shaddix of *Power in the Pulpit*, suggests we read the text prayerfully, carefully, imaginatively, and obediently.[2] In addition to Smith's and Vines's recommendations, I suggest you read the text in various translations: the original biblical language (Hebrew and Greek), a word-for-word (literal) translation

---

1   Robert Smith Jr., *Doctrine That Dances: Bringing Doctrinal Preaching and Teaching to Life* (Nashville: B&H Academic, 2008), 42.
2   Jerry Vines and Jim Shaddix, *Power in the Pulpit: How to Prepare and Deliver Expository Sermons* (Chicago: Moody, 2017), 102–4.

like the NASB or NKJV, a modern language or thought-for-thought (dynamic) like the NIV or NLT, and a free translation like *The Message* or the Living Bible. Reading in different translations will enable you to see numerous perspectives on interpreting the text.

STEP 4: EXEGETE THE PREACHING TEXT

In the book *How to Read the Bible for All Its Worth*, exegesis is defined as "the careful, systematic study of the Scripture to discover the original, intended meaning."[3] You can begin your exegetical study with three simple questions:

> Question 1. What does the text say? (Observation)
> Question 2. What does the text mean? (Interpretation)
> Question 3. How does the text apply to our lives? (Application)

Question 1—What Does the Text Say? (Observation)

The primary question to begin exegesis is, What does the text say? This has to do with observation. When you begin exegesis of the preaching text, you become a detective who is trying to discover the truth or main point of the text. You will discover the truth of the text by looking for six clues and asking six questions. What are the six clues for observing the details of the text?

Clue 1. You must note what is being emphasized in the text. The emphasis may be determined by the amount of space given to a specific subject. For example, Paul emphasized love, prophecy, and tongues in his discussion of spiritual gifts in 1 Corinthians 12–14. Emphasis can also be determined by a stated purpose (Prov. 1:1–4), order (Luke 6:14–16), and movement from lesser to greater or greater to lesser (1 Cor. 12:4–10).

Clue 2. You must observe what is repeated in the text. You should give attention to repeated Scriptures, words, phrases, clauses, characters,

---

3   Gordon D. Fee and Douglass Stuart, *How to Read the Bible for All Its Worth* (Grand Rapids: Zondervan, 2003), 27.

people, incidents, circumstances, and patterns. In John 10:11–18, Jesus repeated words about laying down his life four times. So in preparing a message from these verses, I would want to know why Jesus said it four times.

Old Testament passages mentioned in the New Testament are examples of repeated Scriptures. I would want to know why the person in the New Testament quoted or referenced an Old Testament passage. For example, in Mark 15:34 and Luke 4:19, Jesus quoted Old Testament passages. Another example is Matthew 3:3 in which the author referenced Isaiah 61:1.

Clue 3. You must notice what is related in the text. How do you see this clue in the text? The movement from general to specific in Matthew 6:1–18 is one clue of what is related. The questions and answers in Romans 6 is another clue of what is related. The cause and effect in Romans 8:1–4 is another clue of what is related.

Clue 4. You must spot the comparisons in the text. The biblical authors used similes and metaphors for comparison in their writing. Similes use the words "as" or "like" for comparison (Ps. 42:1). Metaphors do not use the words "like" or "as" for comparison (Ps. 42:3).

Clue 5. You must notice the contrasts in the text. The word "but" is used for contrast. Metaphors can also illustrate contrast. Irony is another form of contrast (1 Cor. 4:7–14).

Clue 6. You must detect life application. This clue helps you observe what the Scripture says about reality and how the Bible connects to everyday life. You should also note how the text relates to your personal experience.

Once you fill in your clues, you may move on to the second part of observation, that is, asking questions. You should ask six questions: who, what, when, where, why, and how. The following are sample questions to ask as you study the text.

Who? Who is the author of the book? Who are the recipients? Who are the main characters in the text?

What? What is the mood of the text? What is the topic? What are the key words? What do the words mean?

When? When was the book written? When did the event happen? When was the prophecy fulfilled?

Where? Where was the book written? Where were the recipients living? Where does this topic appear throughout the Bible?

Why? Why does the author include this material and not other things? Why does he emphasize this topic instead of another topic?

How? How does this text relate to its context? How many times does the author repeat a word or phrase?

You can ask unlimited who, what, when, where, why, and how questions. One time I had an assignment in a preaching course that required me to ask at least twenty-five questions from Acts 1:8.

Question 2—What Does the Text Mean?
(Interpretation)

The second primary question for exegesis is, What does the text mean? This has to do with interpretation. Fee and Stuart give three general principles for exegesis and interpretation: 1) the aim of good interpretation is simple, to get at the plain meaning of the text,[4] 2) the text cannot mean today what it could not mean to the original audience, and 3) when we share commonalities with first-century hearers, the same word applies to us today.[5] You will need five keys to unlock the interpretation of the text to discover its meaning.

---

4   Fee and Stuart, *How to Read the Bible*, 21.
5   Fee and Stuart, *How to Read the Bible*, 74–75.

Key 1: Content. This key is discovered through observing the details of the text. You can refer to your life-changing sermon guide (appendix 1), which will include the details of the text you discovered from the six clues and six questions.

The compilation of information is what you will use to understand the content of the text. In *Living by the Book,* the authors wrote, "The more time you spend in Observation, the less time you will have to spend in Interpretation and the more accurate will be your result. The less time you spend in Observation, the more time you will have to spend in Interpretation, and the less accurate will be your result."[6] So do not rush to interpretation because good observation is critical for accurate interpretation.

In addition to observations gleaned from the six clues and six questions, word studies and understanding the characteristics of the literary genre are important for interpreting the content of the text.

HOW TO DO A WORD STUDY

After observing what the text says, using the six clues and six questions provided in the main text, you may have noticed some words that you must define. Therefore, you will need to do a word study. You want to know the definition of the word used in the original language (either Greek or Hebrew). Why do you have to worry with the word in the original language? You have to know the original language root because English translators use different synonyms for the same Hebrew or Greek words in their translation. Word studies can be relatively simple if you have access to Logos or another Bible study software. However, we do not always have access to software, so here is the old-fashioned word study guide.

---

6   Howard G. Hendricks and William Hendricks, *Living by the Book: The Art and Science of Reading the Bible* (Chicago: Moody, 2007), 229.

Step 1—Select a word. You will have to determine what words are important. For example, what words are emphasized, repeated, related, or alike? From Psalm 150 we will select the word "praise."

Step 2—Use a concordance. A concordance lists every occurrence of a given word in the Bible. Concordances are published according to particular Bible translations. Most translations have a corresponding concordance. For this example, *Strong's Concordance, King James Version* (KJV), will be used.

Step 3—Find the word number. Most concordances are arranged in two sequences. The first sequence is an alphabetical listing of every word in the King James Bible. The second sequence lists every occurrence of that word in order from Genesis to Revelation.

First, look up the word "praise" in the alphabetical entry of words. Under the entry for "praise," run down the verse entries in the canonical order until you come to Psalm 150:1. When you find Psalm 150:1, look at the right of the verse entry and find a number entry. If all you see the ditto mark ("), it means that the word number is the last one entered previously somewhere above in the column.

The word number is part of a word number system coded to the original Hebrew or Greek text. Each distinct word is given a unique number. The number to the right of the verse entry for "praise" in Psalm 150:1 is the number of the particular Hebrew word the translators were translating in that verse. This number coding system in a concordance is what makes you able to access the original language in an English translation.

Step 4—Find the original language word. The code number for the Hebrew word behind the translation "praise" in Psalm 150:1 is 1984. (Trace the "ditto" marks back up the column to the entry for Ps. 149:3.) In the back of *Strong's Concordance* are two dictionaries. The first is a Hebrew dictionary for the Old Testament, and the second is a Greek dictionary for the New Testament. Both dictionaries are arranged numerically from the lowest to highest number. Find the Hebrew dictionary in the back of *Strong's Concordance* and look up the code number for your particular word, in this case "praise." When you find the number 1984, you will see the dictionary entry for your Hebrew word behind "praise" in Psalm 150:1.

First, you will see the actual Hebrew spelling. Next, you will see a transliteration of this Hebrew word, *halal.* (Transliteration is using English letter equivalents for the Hebrew letters to help one read the word in English.) Then, you will see a pronunciation guide with an accent mark to help you say the Hebrew word correctly, *haw-lal.* Finally, you will see a brief definition of this particular word: "to celebrate, commend, praise." This will be a general meaning used only for starters and is not to be used strictly for **every occurrence of the term.**

Step 5—Research the word. Several resources could help here, such as Bible dictionary articles or encyclopedias. One research tool is *Mounce's Complete Expository Dictionary of Old and New Testament Words.* First, in Mounce's dictionary, find the article on "praise." This article is on page 528. According to this article, four Hebrew words are translated as "praise." Find the Hebrew word and Strong's number in this article that corresponds with the word in step 4. This article will tell you how many times this word occurs in the Old Testament and how it is used.

Step 6—Establish the basic range of meanings. According to the concordance and dictionary, *halal* means "to celebrate, commend, praise, boast, and exult." So which word do you use? Your context will determine which word is appropriate.

Key 2: Context. This key refers to where this text fits in the Bible. We must identity four contexts: 1) literary context—words before and after the Scripture text, 2) biblical context—where the passage fits into biblical history, 3) geographical context—the location of the author and recipients of the text, and 4) theological context—what the author and readers understood about God.

Key 3: Comparison. This key compares Scripture with Scripture. The best way to interpret Scripture is with Scripture. You may use cross-references in your Bible. A concordance, *Nave's Topical Bible*, or *The Treasury of Scripture Knowledge* are also good tools to use for cross-referencing Scripture. When searching cross-references, you must be careful to read the cross-references within their contexts as well.

Key 4: Culture. The text was written to a specific group of people who lived in a particular culture. Therefore, we should know the social setting, historical situation, language, customs, and political environment of the text.

Key 5: Consultation. This key involves consulting other resources for interpretation. Once you have studied the text for yourself, you can refer to other resources to gain understanding of the text. The basic resources to consult are a study Bible, Bible dictionary, Bible encyclopedia, dictionary of biblical words, and a commentary. A commentary should be the last resource consulted during interpretation. Reading a commentary prematurely can influence your viewpoint and could limit what you see in the text.

PREACHING FROM DIFFERENT BIBLE GENRES

Following are some practical guidelines on preaching from different Bible genres. The word *genre* refers to the form or style of literature. The Bible is composed of several styles of literature. I classify the genres into six general categories: narrative, wisdom and poetry, prophetic, gospels and the book of Acts, letters, and apocalyptic.

Narrative

The majority of the Bible is narrative literature, which means the Bible is full of stories. I classify Genesis to Esther and Matthew to Acts as narrative literature. Preaching biblical narrative is challenging for many preachers. I hope the following guidelines help you understand how to preach the narrative genre. First, you should identify the "story within the story." Narrative literature is a story; therefore, you should identify the five elements of a story so you can understand and apply the Scripture you are preaching. Each story has characters, a setting, and a plot, which includes the conflict and resolution.

The typical characters in a story are the protagonist (hero of the story) and antagonist (the person or group who opposes the protagonist). The protagonist is the problem solver and the antagonist may be the troublemaker. You should develop a profile of the characters. What is the character's name, family history, physical attributes, personal traits, and relationship with God? Do not overlook the supporting characters in the story. You will also want to address the setting, the location of the story. The majority of the sermon may focus on the plot. The plot includes the events of the story, that is, the beginning (conflict), the middle (climax), and the end (conclusion).

Sometimes we reconstruct the story to fit a "three-point" sermon structure. However, these narratives were not written to be preached or taught in three points. Therefore, I believe it is important to follow the flow of the Scripture. It is like riding down a river on a kayak or boat. You follow the flow of the river to get to your destination. As the captain of the ship, you point out the various landmarks along the journey. So it is with the narrative genre. Follow the natural flow of Scripture to your destination. As you take your audience through the journey, you may highlight some truths, illustrations, or personal applications on the way to your destination. Your sermon structure may be more inductive than deductive. This means you share the main point at the end of the message rather than at the beginning of the message.

Within the narrative genre, you will find what is called the law books, also called the Pentateuch (five books) or the "books of Moses"—that is, Genesis, Exodus, Leviticus, Numbers, and Deuteronomy. How do we interpret the laws in the Old Testament? First, we must understand the intent behind the whole law. For example, the laws of Leviticus 17–26 may not apply to us today, but the principle remains the same. God wanted his people to be holy. He wanted them to set themselves apart for him. God demands the same of us today. He wants us to be holy and to separate ourselves from the ungodly things of this world. Second, we must be able to discern which laws can be directly applied to us today, and which laws cannot be directly applied or correlated to our current society. The latter may include certain dietary or ceremonial laws. Third, we must relate the laws to our Christian faith. For example, a lesson on the Passover can help us to understand the Lord's Supper.[a]

Wisdom and Poetry

I classify Job through Songs of Solomon as wisdom and poetry. Job, Proverbs, and Ecclesiastes are wisdom books. Psalms and Songs of Solomon are poetry books.

You will find great applications in all of these books. For the wisdom books you want to search for truths relating to God, yourself, and life. For example, the Proverbs were written to encourage the readers to discipline themselves to live a righteous life and to discern words of wisdom for understanding and life application. Also, Proverbs are principles not promises. I hear parents quote Proverbs 22:6 when their children have grown up to become someone different than the parents imagined. Although Proverbs 22:6 is true, it is a principle, not a promise.

For the poetry books you want to identify the poetic structure or features of the Scripture. Hebrew poetry does not rhyme with sound. Instead, most of it uses parallel statements or ideas. Psalms have three primary types of parallelisms: synonyms, contrasts, and explanation. Parallelisms can also amplify a previous thought. Read Psalm 24:2 and notice the synonyms. The author repeats the same thought in the second line that was stated in the first line. Read Psalm 1:6 and notice that the second line contrasts the statement of the first line. Read Psalm 2:6 and Psalm 130:4 and notice how the second line explains or gives more information about the first line. Read Psalm 1:1 and notice how the second line amplifies the thought of the first line.[b] In addition to identifying the poetic features, many of the psalms follow a similar three-part structure: prayer, problem, and praise. For example, Psalm 4 opens with a prayer (verse 1), discusses the problem (verses 2–7), and concludes with a praise (verse 8).

Prophetic

After the wisdom and poetry books, you will find the Prophets (Isaiah to Malachi). Oftentimes we divide these books into two main categories: Major Prophets (Isaiah to Ezekiel) and Minor Prophets (Hosea to Malachi). These categories can be misleading. You might think the Major Prophets were more important than the Minor Prophets in Israelite history. The Major Prophets are major because of the size of the book, not the significance of their ministry. Even though the messages of the Minor Prophets were shorter, they were just as important as the longer messages of the Major Prophets, and the ramifications for disobedience to God were the same.

One key to understanding the Prophets is determining if the prophecy was forthtelling or foretelling. *Forthtelling* means the message was addressing an issue in the lives of the prophet's audience. God wanted to correct their behavior or attitudes. *Foretelling* refers to a message that depicts a future event or outcome. So what does forthtelling and foretelling mean to us? Forthtelling means the message was time specific. The prophecy was for that moment. However, we can still apply the timeless principles of the prophecy to our congregations. Foretelling means the message was fulfilled later or is still waiting to be fulfilled. With these messages we must determine if the fulfillment relates to us as the church or specifically to Israel as the "people of God."

Before moving to New Testament genres, I want to give a summary statement for preaching from Old Testament literature. In 1 Corinthians 10:6–11, the apostle Paul writes,

> Now these things happened as examples for us, so that we would not crave evil things as they also craved. Do not be idolaters, as some of them were; as it is written, "The people sat down to eat and drink, and stood up to play." Nor let us act immorally, as some of them did, and twenty-three thousand fell in one day. Nor let us try the Lord, as some of them did, and were destroyed by the serpents. Nor grumble, as some of them did, and were destroyed by the destroyer. Now these things happened to them as an example, and they were written for our instruction, upon whom the ends of the ages have come.

Some preachers consider the Old Testament irrelevant for Christians because of the "outdated" laws and prophecies. However, Paul was writing to Christians when he penned that statement. Just like the Corinthians, we can learn from the examples in the Old Testament too.

Gospels and Acts

Once you flip over to the New Testament, you will find the gospels and the book of Acts. The principles of narrative can apply to these five books as well. However, I have some additional thoughts on preaching from these books. When reading the Gospels, you should try to understand what the writer is trying to convey about Jesus to his audience.

Many times I hear preachers refer to the Gospels as biographies about Jesus. Though this statement is true, the Gospels were not written to explain in great details the birth, early life, adolescent years, adulthood, and death of Jesus Christ. The four gospel writers had a unique purpose when telling their story regarding the life and ministry of Jesus. So when preaching from the Gospels, you want to understand the author's perspective. For example, Matthew focuses on the message of Jesus. Matthew depicts Jesus as a king. The opening chapters prove the royal lineage of Jesus and the closing chapter illustrates his kingly authority. Therefore, you would be preaching from Matthew as if you are delivering a message for the King of kings. Actually, all of our sermons are messages we are delivering for the King of kings. However, when preaching from Matthew, you want to see the teaching of Jesus as an edict, an official statement from the person in authority.

In Mark's gospel, the writer focuses on the ministry of Jesus. Mark's gospel is action-packed. Mark skips the birth of Jesus and begins with his ministry. Luke's gospel focuses on the humanity of Jesus. Luke demonstrates how Jesus interacted with various people in his world, especially minorities, outcasts, and the poor. John's gospel highlights the majesty of Jesus. John wanted his readers to see Jesus as God in the flesh.

When applying the gospels or any narrative to your audience, you should encourage them to find themselves in the story. Ask your audience if they are the disciples, the Pharisees, or the crowd of people in the Scripture. For example, would they be the sinner asking for forgiveness, the parent asking Jesus to heal the child, the blind person asking for sight, or the little boy giving up his lunch?

In the Acts of the Apostles, the title speaks for itself. The books is about the acts of the apostles, the work they continued to do after the ascension of Jesus. Be careful when preaching Acts, especially when referencing church practices. Acts serves as a model for the church. So you want to draw principles for what we can do today rather than focus on specific precepts or practices, which may not transfer into our culture or time period.

Letters

Once you leave the Acts of the Apostles, you will find the letters (Romans to Jude). Some classify this literature as "letters and epistles." A letter would be written to a specific audience or recipient like Romans and 1 Timothy, whereas an epistle would be written to a general audience like James or 1 Peter. Here are some guidelines on preaching from the letters. First, be aware of which parts of the letter your text falls within. Most letters have six parts: 1) author, 2) recipients, 3) greeting, 4) prayer, 5) body, and 6) final greetings and farewell.[c] Second, you must identify and understand the purpose or reason the letter was written. Some letters were written to correct behavior. Other letters were written to address doctrinal issues or provide clarity on certain topics.[d] Third, you should identify and preach the author's complete thought on a subject. Most of the time this means you should preach a paragraph or multiple paragraphs to convey the author's entire thought on a subject. Fourth, look for the imperatives in your preaching text. The imperative will probably be the main point of the text and the major points will intersect with it. Therefore, the imperative should be the main point of the sermon, and the sermon points should intersect with it through explanation, illustration, or application.

Apocalyptic

The last genre is apocalyptic literature: the book of Revelation. The principles of preaching from the letters applies to chapters 1–3, and the principles of preaching from the prophets applies to chapters 4–22. Here are some general principles to keep in mind when preaching Revelation. First, the figurative language was used to conceal the message from the secular Romans, but it revealed the message to the persecuted Christians who read it. Therefore, any interpretation of the text must have been discernible and relevant to the original audience. Second, the overarching message is that God will be victorious over evil, a judgment day is coming for the righteous and unrighteous,[e] and Christians will enjoy the presence of God forever in his new heaven and new earth. Therefore, It is important to remember to keep your eyes—and those of your congregation—on the main points of the book rather than getting lost in the details. Third, don't let your theology drive your interpretation, let the interpretation drive your theology. It is okay to be a have a premillennial or postmillennial theology; however, don't force theology into every Scripture. This principle is also true for all genres of Scripture. Don't force your theology or doctrine into the text. Fourth, interpret the text as literally as possible. Although Revelation is filled with symbolism and figurative language, not every Scripture is an allegory. Some Scriptures mean exactly what is written.

a. Harold Bryson, *Expository Preaching: The Art of Preaching through a Book of the Bible* (Nashville: B&H, 1995), 207–9.

b. Bryson, *Expository Preaching*, 217–18.

c. Gordon D. Fee and Douglass Stuart, *How to Read the Bible for All Its Worth* (Grand Rapids: Zondervan, 2003), 56–57.

d. Fee and Stuart, *How to Read the Bible*, 58.

e. Bryson, *Expository Preaching*, 282–83.

Question 3—How Does the Text Apply to Our Lives (Application)?

The third primary question for step 4 (exegesis) is, How does the text apply to our lives? Good exegesis is necessary because misinterpretation leads to misapplication. Application is important: we need to understand how to put the Scripture into action because *the key to spiritual growth is living what you learn.* Life-changing application can be identified by asking five simple questions. I call these "FAITH" questions.

- Forgiveness: Do you have any sins to confess?
- Attitude and Actions: What attitude or actions will you try to change?
- Insight and Instruction: What did you learn from the Scripture?
- Thanksgiving: Did you see any reasons to praise God?
- Helping Others: What did you see that could encourage someone else?

I will discuss more on life-changing applications in the next chapter.

RIGHTLY DIVIDING THE WORD OF TRUTH

Dr. Chuck Swindoll is a life-changing preacher who makes every effort to rightly divide the Word of Truth. Swindoll is the senior pastor of Stonebriar Community Church in Frisco, Texas, and served as president of Dallas Theological Seminary from 1994 to 2001. His sermons are broadcast in all fifty states and more than 2,100 media outlets through the Insight for Living broadcast.[7] In 1996 and 2018, Baylor University identified Swindoll as one of the twelve most effective preachers in the English-speaking world.[8] Since 1963, Chuck

---

7   "Chuck Swindoll," Insight for Living Ministries, accessed January 31, 2021, https://www.insight.org/about/chuck-swindoll.

8   "Baylor University's Truett Seminary Announces 12 Most Effective Preachers in English-Speaking World," Baylor University, May 1, 2018, https://www.baylor.edu/mediacommunications/news.php?action=story&story=198528.

Swindoll has used the same Bible study techniques and principles you learned in this chapter. He learned these skills from the late Howard Hendricks while attending Dallas Theological Seminary. According to Swindoll, "Not a week passes without my returning to those tried-and-true guidelines I imbibed decades ago. To this day, I have not delivered a sermon, conducted a teaching session, released a broadcast or podcast, or given a brief devotional without first putting those principles to use."[9]

Why are people eager to listen to Swindoll's sermons? People are eager to hear Swindoll's sermons because he rightly divides the Word of Truth. Swindoll takes Paul's challenge to Timothy seriously and works hard to explain the Bible accurately.

WORDS OF WISDOM

Dr. Tony Evans is a life-changing preacher who is the founder and senior pastor of Oak Cliff Bible Fellowship in Dallas and founder and president of The Urban Alternative. He has written more than one hundred books, booklets, and Bible studies. Dr. Evans was the first African American to earn a doctorate of theology from Dallas Theological Seminary. In 2018, he was named one of the twelve most effective preachers in the English-speaking world by Baylor University. Dr. Evans holds the honor of writing and publishing the first full-Bible commentary and study Bible by an African American. His radio broadcast, *The Alternative with Dr. Tony Evans*, can be heard on more than 1,400 radio outlets daily and in more than 130 countries.[10]

In his book *The Power of Preaching: Crafting a Creative Expository Sermon*, Dr. Evans writes these words of wisdom to encourage preachers in our study of the Scriptures:

---

9   Charles R. Swindoll, *Searching the Scriptures: Find the Nourishment Your Soul Needs* (Carol Stream, IL: Tyndale, 2017), xii.

10   "Dr. Tony Evans," TonyEvans.org, accessed January 31, 2021, https://tonyevans.org.

Ezra 7:10 is one of the fundamental descriptions of who a preacher is. Memorize this verse. Let it be your definition as a preacher. . . . If you follow Ezra's lead (which I hope you do), you will discover that preaching is first and foremost for yourself. Instead of studying and preaching for someone else, study and preach for yourself while letting others in on what you learn. This changes why you go into the study. You are now not just going into your study time because your church or class needs a sermon or lesson. You are also going in to ask God to teach you. This gives you a different mindset. Like Ezra, you will study in order to first put what you've learned into practice. Then you will teach what you've learned. You will find when you approach your preaching from this perspective that your sermons begin to feel more authentic and genuine than before. They will resonate with your audience at a deeper heart-level than before. You will desire to live and proclaim biblical truth in such a way that the spiritual principle and application takes root in the hearers and in yourself, enabling the Holy Spirit to produce ongoing growth.[11]

Are you serious about rightly dividing the Scriptures? Exegesis is not easy; it is hard work. You cannot be lazy and do good exegesis. You must be disciplined and diligent because "the Bible does not yield its truth to lazy minds."[12] Be like Chuck Swindoll and be diligent in observing, interpreting, and applying the Bible accurately. Be like Tony Evans (and Ezra) by studying the Word for yourself first and foremost.

---

11 Tony Evans, *The Power of Preaching: Crafting a Creative Expository Sermon* (Chicago: Moody, 2019), 22–23.
12 Swindoll, *Searching the Scriptures*, 17.

CHAPTER 4

STRUCTURING THE SERMON

How do you organize your sermons? Do you use a deductive or inductive approach? Maybe you use a hybrid of both. Do you use the traditional "three points and a poem" method? Or do you prefer a more contemporary method?

My sermon structure has varied over the past twenty years. I was fourteen years old when I started preaching in my freshman year of high school. During this stage of ministry, my sermon structure was like an English essay. I had an introduction, several paragraphs in my body, and a conclusion.

In college, my sermon structure evolved in three stages. During my freshman year at Alabama State University, a historic black college and university in Montgomery, my sermon structure resembled a history report. Because I was a history major, each sermon included an emphasis on the background and culture of the preaching text. I still employed the essay structure, but my transitions between points and paragraphs usually answered a who, what, when, where, why, or how question.

In my sophomore year, I read Haddon Robinson's book *Biblical Preaching: The Development and Delivery of Expository Messages*. It was the first book I had read on expository preaching. This book introduced me to the concept of the Big Idea or having one main point for the sermon. This *one main point* concept gave my sermon structure more unity. This book was a little too weighty for me, as a sophomore in college, to digest fully without someone guiding me through it. So I put it on the shelf for a few years.

During my senior year of college at Selma University, a historic black college and university for ministers in Selma, Alabama, I also began pastoring my first church, Saint Peter Missionary Baptist Church in Abbeville. I read several books by revered African American preachers, such as *A Certain Sound of the Trumpet: Crafting a Sermon of Authority*, by Samuel DeWitt Proctor; *Designing the Sermon: Order and Movement in Preaching*, by James Earl Massey; *We Have This Ministry: The Heart of the Pastor's Vocation*, by Gardner Taylor and Samuel DeWitt Proctor; and several works by James Cone. From Proctor, I used the thesis-antithesis to build tension and gain the audience's attention through my introduction. From Massey, I learned to let the Scripture influence my sermon outline rather than superimposing my structure over the Scripture. Taylor and Proctor encouraged me to include a pastor's heart in my structure. Cone challenged me to exhort and encourage the audience in the midst of their adversity.

While taking my first preaching class at New Orleans Baptist Theological Seminary, I was introduced to a traditional way of structuring a sermon. This outline includes the central proposition of the text (CPT), central proposition of the sermon (CPS), purpose of the sermon in a sentence (PSS), a key word (KW), a transitional sentence (TS), an introduction, main points, and a conclusion. In order to keep things simple for me and the preachers I train, instead of using CPT, CPS, and PSS, I use the main point of the text (MPT), the life-changing principle (LCP), and the purpose of the sermon (POS).

The fourth step for preaching a life-changing sermon is *structuring the sermon*. *Studying the Scripture* lays a foundation for the sermon; *structuring the sermon* builds the message's framework. The structure of the biblical message has three basic parts: an introduction, the body (exposition), and a conclusion. So what is the first step for structuring the sermon?

STEP 1: THE MAIN POINT

The first step for structuring the sermon is discovering the main point of the text (MPT). Though the preacher may identify several ideas in the text, the biblical author had one primary purpose or point in writing the Scripture. He had one main idea or central truth that he communicated to the readers. Your task is to identify the author's main point. The main point of the text is discovered by answering two questions: What is the subject? and What is the author saying about the subject? After answering those two questions, you will have the subject of the text and its complement, and you can answer the third question: What is the main point of the text? You should write a complete sentence using the subject and complement to form the main point of the text.

Let's practice discovering the main point of the text. Read 1 Corinthians 12:27–31:

> Now you are Christ's body, and individually members of it. And God has appointed in the church, first apostles, second prophets, third teachers, then miracles, then gifts of healings, helps, administrations, various kinds of tongues. All are not apostles, are they? All are not prophets, are they? All are not teachers, are they? All are not workers of miracles, are they? All do not have gifts of healings, do they? All do not speak with tongues, do they? All do not interpret, do they? But earnestly desire the greater gifts.

1. What is the subject? *Gifts in the church.*
2. What is the author saying about the subject? *Paul is talking about how the gifts were appointed by God and that the Corinthians should pursue greater gifts.*
3. What is the main point of the text (MPT)? *Paul encouraged the Corinthians to desire the greater gifts.*

Now you try it! Read 1 Corinthians 12:1–11.

1. What is the subject?
2. What is the author saying about subject?
3. What is the main point of the text (MPT)?

Read 1 Corinthians 12:12–26.

1. What is the subject?
2. What is the author saying about subject?
3. What is the main point of the text (MPT)?

STEP 2: THE TEXTUAL OUTLINE

After discovering the main point of the text, you will complete the second step, which is creating an exegetical or textual outline of the Scripture. This outline is the skeleton or basic structure of the sermon. This outline includes the main point of the text (MPT), major points, and subpoints. Usually your statement and points are written in the past tense.

Textual Outline of 1 Corinthians 12:27–31

MPT: Paul encouraged the Corinthians to desire the greater gifts.

Outline:

I. God gave gifts to the church, the body of Christ (v. 27–28).
    a. God gave the church speaking gifts: apostles, prophets, teachers, and tongues.
    b. God gave the church serving gifts: miracles, healings, helps, and administrations.
II. Paul asked a series of rhetorical questions about the various gifts (v. 29–30).
    a. Paul implied all of them were not gifted with all of the speaking gifts.
    b. Paul implied all of them were not gifted with all of the serving gifts.

III. Paul told them to earnestly desire the greater gifts.
   a. Paul told them how to pursue the gifts.
   b. Paul told them which gifts to pursue.

Now you try it! Using the format of the textual outline above, create your own outlines of both 1 Corinthians 12:1–11 and 1 Corinthians 12:12–26.

STEP 3: THE SERMON OUTLINE

The third step is developing the sermon outline from the textual outline. You will contemporize your textual outline by writing the main point of the text (MPT), major points, and subpoints in the present tense. The contemporizing of your MPT now becomes the life-changing principle (LCP) of the sermon.

The Life-Changing Principle (LCP)

The LCP is the bridge from the biblical world to the preacher's modern context. The LCP makes the biblical text speak to the contemporary audience. For example, if the MPT is "Paul commanded Timothy to preach the Word," then the LCP could be "We must be faithful to preach God's Word." Try to keep the sentence to less than ten words and definitely no more than fifteen. This helps with your clarity and the audience's memorization of the sermon's main point. Notice how many words I use for the MPT and LCP.

MPT: Paul encouraged the Corinthians to pursue the greater gifts.
LCP: Every Christian should desire the greater gifts.

You will follow the same process for converting the points of the text to the sermon points. The sermon points should be stated in the present or future tense. The sermon points should connect to the LCP. The sermon points answer a what, why, or how question. *What* questions inform the congregation. *Why* questions motivate the congregation. *How* questions give practical instructions to the congregation.

Points of the Text (1 Corinthians 12:27-31)

I. God gave gifts to the church, the body of Christ (vv. 27–28).
   a. God gave the church speaking gifts: apostles, prophets, teachers, and tongues.
   b. God gave the church serving gifts: miracles, healings, helps, and administrations.
II. Paul asked a series of rhetorical questions about the various gifts (vv. 29–30).
   a. Paul implied all of them were not gifted with all of the speaking gifts.
   b. Paul implied all of them were not gifted with all of the serving gifts.
III. Paul told them to earnestly desire the greater gifts.
   a. Paul told them how to pursue the gifts.
   b. Paul told them which gifts to pursue.

Sermon Points

I. God designates gifts in the church (vv. 27–28).
   a. The church has speaking gifts: apostles, prophets, teachers, and tongues.
   b. The church has serving gifts: miracles, healings, helps, and administrations.
II. We do not all have the same gifts (vv. 29–30).
   a. We are not gifted with all of the speaking gifts.
   b. We are not gifted with all of the serving gifts.
III. We must desire the greater gifts (vv. 29–31).
   a. We must learn how to pursue the gifts.
   b. We must learn which gifts to pursue.

How does the preacher unify the LCP and the sermon points? Some preachers use a key word to unify the sermons. For example, "We will notice three *reasons* Christians should desire the greater gifts." The key word is *reasons*. Therefore, each sermon point will be a reason for obeying the LCP. The number of key words is unlimited. One key word to avoid is "things." Three common key words are reasons, truths, and ways. Other preachers may use questions to connect the LCP to the sermon points. For example, who designates the gifts, what are our gifts, and what gifts should we pursue?

STEP 4: THE EXPOSITION

The fourth step in structuring the sermon is writing the exposition, also known as the body of the sermon. The exposition has three parts: 1) explanation, 2) illustration, and 3) application.

Explanation: Placing God's Word into People's Heads

The first part of exposition is explanation. Explanation places God's Word into people's heads. The purpose of explanation is to make the text plain or clear for the audience. Good exegesis is essential for explanation. The preacher must exegete the context, meaning, and significance of the Scripture to explain the meaning of the biblical text. You can refer to your notes from the exegetical study for this information. You should explain the historical context and the meaning of key words or phrases. You should explain what the passage meant in the original context and what it means for your contemporary audience.

How does the preacher decide which details to include in the sermon? I ask three questions to help me select the material for the sermon. First, "What will help the audience understand the main point?" Second, "What does the audience need to know or understand about the main point?" Third, "What questions may the audience have about the text or main point?"

Illustration: Placing God's Word into People's Hearts

The second part of the exposition is illustration. After you explain the text, you illustrate it. Illustrations place God's Word into people's hearts. An illustration will give the audience a visual of the main point. Illustrations are examples used for clarifying the main point or sermon point.

I have various sources for my illustrations. Once source is everyday observation. I observe people and their behavior as I go through my daily activities. Sometimes I can make an illustration from what I see people do.

Stories are another source for illustrations. When retelling a story, it is important to be a good storyteller. One of the strengths of African American preaching is the art of narration. I use stories from the Bible as illustrations of how we should respond to God's call or chastisement. I use stories from history. I was a history major during my first three years of undergraduate studies, so I have a reservoir of stories from United States history and world history that can be related to my contemporary audience. I also read various biographies growing up. My first biography was on Martin Luther King Jr. in third grade, followed by the autobiography of Malcolm X in fourth grade. I like to use stories from black history. I especially like to highlight Christians in black history. These stories introduce my audience to heroes of the faith they can relate to through culture or experience. For example, the civil rights movement was organized and led by black Christians. I like to use other stories from church history as well. Stories from church history enable me to introduce my congregation to people they never knew existed. For example, I have used George Mueller as an illustration when preaching on prayer.

I also use stories from my personal life. I like to share stories about my family and friends. I have an unlimited list of stories from this group. If I use stories where I'm the main character, I am not always the hero. I never use a story that will embarrass anyone in my circle of family and friends. Sometimes I use stories from previous ministries. These stories usually surround a person's faithfulness or God's answer to prayer. I usually request permission to use these stories, and I may change their name or not use it at all.

Sometimes I use a fictitious story or scenario. I usually start the story with "Imagine this . . ." so that my listeners will know that the story is not a true story but fictitious. Why so many stories? People like stories. People can relate to stories, especially the characters. People remember stories.

I also use sports as illustrations. I have used illustrations of Michael Jordan and LeBron James on leadership. I have used illustrations about Michael Vick and Ray Lewis on choosing friends wisely. I have talked about the salaries of star athletes and coaches in relation to the importance of being a difference maker. I often use sports as an illustration to summarize the book of Revelation. The book of Revelation is like watching a football or basketball game for the second or third time. You already know who won, but you still go through the highs and lows of the game. You celebrate the touchdowns and chastise the turnovers. Like watching the replay of a game, we already know the end of the story for Christians. We are victorious. So now we are just going through the highs and lows of living in this world until we reach our final destination. I also use scenes or quotes from movies, television shows, books, or social media. I may play the scene or display a quote on the screen to stimulate the visual senses.

I also like to use songs: hymns, gospel, contemporary Christian music, and so on. Sometimes I may use secular music, but I don't want my audience to be distracted. Sometimes I can tell the story associated with the song. For example, I have told the story associated with "Amazing Grace," "What a Friend We Have in Jesus," and "Precious Lord."

Application: Placing God's Word into People's Hands

The third part of exposition is application. Application is important because it makes the text practical. The application places God's Word into people's hands. The application will build a bridge from the biblical world to the preacher's modern-day context. Good applications enable the audience to see how the Scriptures work in their lives and everyday context.

I consider the application to be the most overlooked portion of the biblical messages. Sometimes I include applications throughout the sermon. Other times I may put several applications in the conclusion. Below are nine principles for discerning the application points of a life-changing sermon.

1. Applications should be theological. They should help the congregation become more like God. In life-changing sermons, applications encourage the audience to look, live, and love like Jesus Christ. Two questions are good for this type of application. First, "What does God expect of us?" And second, "What would Jesus do?" Answering these two questions will encourage the congregation to conform their attitudes and actions to that of God the Father and God the Son, Jesus Christ.

2. Applications should be clearly formulated at the time of writing the sermon. You should write out the application points and jot down your thoughts so you can include a reference to your applications in the sermon outline. Extemporaneous applications can be relevant but can lack clarity. Writing the applications helps you focus on the details of the application and prevents you from sounding redundant.

3. Applications should be biblical. You should challenge the audience to live the Word of God. The congregation should be hearers and doers of the Word. Therefore, the application must be Scripture-based. You should show the audience how the application relates to the text.

4. Applications should be adaptable. You should address the audience's life in several ways. The preacher can apply the Scriptures to their personal life, family life, church life, work life, and community life.

5. Applications should be universal. Application principles should work in America, Africa, Asia, and Australia. If the application cannot be universal, the preacher should question it before using it.

6. Applications should be visible. You must practice what you preach. You should not be surprised if the congregation does not apply the Word to their lives because they do not see you living the Word in your life.

7. Applications can be statements or principles with specific action. Applications can also be given as a series of questions.

8. Applications should be practical and doable. For example, encouraging the congregation to read the Bible is doable; reading the whole bible in four days, while doable, is not practical.

9. Applications should be contextual. You should consider the people's needs when developing sermon applications. I think of needs in the following seven categories: social, emotional, mental, spiritual, relational, financial, and physical. You can also use questions based on the FAITH acronym to develop application points.

- Forgiveness—Do you have any sins to confess?
- Attitude and Actions—How will you try to change?
- Insight and Instruction—What did you learn from today's Scripture reading?
- Thanksgiving—Did you see any reason to praise God?
- Helping Others—What did you see today that could encourage someone else?

STEP 5: INTRODUCTION AND CONCLUSION

The fifth step of structuring the sermon is writing the introduction and conclusion. The length of my introduction depends on my audience and the subject of the sermon. If I'm preaching through a book of the Bible, I will usually keep my introduction brief because the congregation should be familiar with the historical background and cultural context. My introduction will include an attention getter. I may use a question, quote, or story. My introduction will also include the MPT (main point of the text) and the LCP (life-changing principle).

The introduction can include a transitional sentence, moving you smoothly from one element of the sermon to the next. The transitional sentence from the introduction to the body will include the key word, if a key word is used. You will also use a transitional sentence to shift from one major point to another. The following statements are examples of transitional sentences.

Transition from introduction to sermon point:
Let's look at some ways to love the Lord wholeheartedly. The first
way to love the Lord wholeheartedly is by distinguishing the person
of God.

**Transition from first sermon point to second sermon
point:**
After distinguishing the person of God, the second way to love the
Lord wholeheartedly is by devoting your entire being to him.

**Transition from second sermon point to third sermon
point:**
After devoting your entire being to the Lord, the third way to love
the Lord wholeheartedly is by dedicating yourself to memorizing his
commands.

The conclusion has three sections. The first section summarizes the
sermon and includes the MPT, LCP, and sermon points. The second
section calls the audience to action with an application. The third
section encourages saints to celebrate God's glory and invites sinners
to surrender their life to Christ through an invitation.

STEP 6: THE TITLE

The sixth step in structuring the sermon is selecting a title. The title
should be based on the sermon topic. For some biblical messages, the
sermon title may be the main point of the sermon. The sermon title
is an invitation to the congregation to explore God's Word with you.
The title can be an attention-getter or build suspense.[1] The sermon
should live up to the title.

STEP 7: THE FINAL SERMON OUTLINE

The seventh step of structuring the sermon is completing the sermon
outline. My sermon outline will include the title, text, subject of the

---

1   Charlie Dates, *Say It! Celebrating Expository Preaching in the African American
     Tradition*, ed. Eric C. Redmond (Chicago: Moody, 2020) 18.

sermon, MPT, LCP, key word (KW), purpose of the sermon (POS), transitional sentence (TS) from the introduction to the body of the sermon, full introduction, sermon points, illustration ideas, application ideas, and full conclusion with invitation. Below is an example.

Title: Desire the Greater Gifts
Text: 1 Corinthians 12:27–31
Subject: Spiritual Gifts
MPT: Paul encouraged the Corinthians to pursue the greater gifts.
LCP: However, it is imperative for Christians to desire the greater gifts.
POS: Hearers will begin to pursue the greater gifts.
KW: Reasons
TS: We will notice three reasons Christians should desire the greater gifts.

Introduction
What gifts do you desire? Do you want the gift of prophecy, administration, knowledge, or tongues? When we read today's Scripture, we notice that Paul encouraged the Corinthians to pursue the greater gifts. Christians knowing their spiritual gifts is a big concern for the contemporary church. It is important for Christians to know their spiritual gifts. However, it is imperative for Christians to desire the greater gifts. Now let's turn our attention to what the apostle Paul wrote to the Corinthians. We will notice three reasons Christians should desire the greater gifts.

Sermon Points

I. God designates gifts in the church (1 Cor. 12:27–28).
   a. The church has speaking gifts: apostles, prophets, teachers, and tongues.
   b. The church has serving gifts: miracles, healings, helps, and administrations.
II. We do not all have the same gifts (1 Cor. 12:29–30).
   a. We are not gifted with all of the speaking gifts.
   b. We are not gifted with all of the serving gifts.

III. We must desire the greater gifts (1 Corinthians 12:29–31).
   a.   We must learn how to pursue the gifts.
   b.   We must learn which gifts to pursue.

Conclusion

What gifts do you desire? *Paul encouraged the Corinthians to pursue the greater gifts* from the list he provided to them. It is important for Christians to know their spiritual gifts; *however, it is imperative for Christians to desire the greater gifts.* I hope you desire the greater gifts. And the greatest gift we can desire is Jesus Christ. Jesus is God's gift to us. God has given Jesus to us, but will you receive him today?

Illustration ideas: The human body has greater parts and lesser parts.

Application ideas: Having a greater gift does not make one a greater Christian.

Variations of Sermon Structures

After twenty-plus years of preaching, I try to structure sermons in the best way to convey the truth of the text to my audience so they can understand it and apply it to their lives. Therefore, not all of my sermon structures or outlines are in a traditional format. Over the years, I have developed several different structures or outlines I can use for a biblical message. I include sermons and outlines in this book to demonstrate the various possibilities I use for preaching a biblical message.

The most frequent format I use is the Rhetorical or Traditional sermon outline. Some have called this the "three points and a poem" structure. Usually I have two to five points, and I don't conclude with a poem. I use the format for preaching from letters.

Another sermon structure I use is the Question-Answer outline. The sermon points are presented as questions, and the exposition of the sermons answer those questions. I use this for evangelistic, apologetic, and doctrinal sermons. I believe it can also be used for any genre of Scripture.

A third sermon style is the Then-Now format. This sermon has two parts. In part 1, the *then*, I explain the text. In part 2, *the now*, I illustrate the text and provide life application. I have used this method for the genres of narrative and prophecy.

Another sermon structure is the Key Word sermon. In this sermon, I highlight key words in the text. I explain those words in their context and how the words connect to the main point of the sermon. I have used this sermon style for wisdom literature, poetry, prophecy, and letters.

I also use a Devotional structure. This style can be more like a homily or a running commentary with exegetical insights and life application. I use this style for preaching the Psalms or sharing devotional messages.

SERMON ARCHITECTS

Why is it important to structure the sermon? David Martyn Lloyd-Jones, also called the "Doctor," answers this question in his classic book on preaching, *Preaching and Preachers*. The Doctor was a Welsh Protestant minister and medical doctor. He was influential in the British evangelical movement in the twentieth century. He served as the minister of Westminster Chapel for almost thirty years. In *Preaching and Preachers*, Lloyd-Jones writes, "As far as I am concerned if my sermon is not clear and ordered in my mind I cannot preach it to others. I suppose I could stand up and talk, but that would probably muddle people rather than help them. That is why I regard this ordering and shaping of the sermon as most important, and I advocate that you should struggle with this until you get it into shape."[2]

He also writes that he would postpone preaching a sermon if he was not satisfied with its structure: "Rather than ruin something which one feels is going to be better than usual, or mar it or deliver it

---

2   David Martyn Lloyd-Jones, *Preaching and Preachers: The Classic Text with Essays from Mark Dever, Kevin DeYoung, Timothy Keller, John Piper, and Others* (Grand Rapids: Zondervan, 2011), 224.

imperfectly, I put it aside for the moment. I have put such a message aside for a week or a fortnight or even longer. I have then come back to it; and it is only when I have finally satisfied myself as to the shape and form that I have preached it."[3]

Another notable sermon architect was Dr. E. K.Bailey, a prominent black expository preacher during the last thirty years of the twentieth century. Dr. Bailey was the founder of Concord Baptist Church in Dallas, Texas and E. K. Bailey Expository Preaching Conference. In 2010, Dr. Bailey was named one of the twenty-five most influential preachers in the past twenty-five years.[4]

Dr. Bailey's sermon structure consisted of an introduction, main points, and a conclusion. His introductions had definite and variable elements. The definite elements included touching on the text, the subject, and the congregation's need for the message. Bailey's variable elements included the following: the text's biblical background, personal experiences, illustrations, shocking statements, or quotations. Bailey employed variable elements to hook the audience into the message. He used the same methods for the conclusion.[5]

Bailey arranged his sermon according to the text's structure. Sometimes he utilized what he called designed jewel sermons and twin sermons. The jewel sermon looked at the numerous facets of the text. This sermon may highlight a word, phrase, or verse. The twin sermon focused on the positive (what to do) and negative (what not to do) aspects of the text. Many people remember Bailey for his narrative structure of exposition. One of the best examples of this structure is demonstrated in his sermon entitled "The Preacher and the Hoochie."[6] Bailey practiced systematic exposition, preaching through

---

3   Lloyd Jones, *Preaching and Preachers*, 225.
4   Wayne E. Croft, "E.K. Bailey: Expositor of the Word," *Preaching*, accessed December 19, 2020, https://www.preaching.com/articles/past-masters/e-k-bailey-expositor-of-the-word.
5   E.K. Bailey and Warren Wiersbe, *Preaching in Black and White* (Grand Rapids: Zondervan, 2013), 85.
6   See www.sheilab.org for Dr. E. K. Bailey's sermon books and manuscripts.

Bible books in the beginning of his ministry. In the latter years, he preached topical expository sermons to address contemporary issues from a biblical point of view.[7]

WORDS OF WISDOM

In 2018, Dr. Ralph Douglas West was identified by Baylor University as one of the most effective preachers in the English-speaking world. He is the founder and senior pastor of The Church Without Walls in Houston, Texas. The church began with thirty-two members and now serves 24,000-plus families. Dr. West serves on the faculty of Truett Seminary.[8] He also hosts the IC3 Church Growth and Development Conference.

In an interview with *Preaching* magazine, Dr. West answered a question related to preparing an effective application.

> I borrow something Haddon Robinson said he does. He says he looks into the faces of what he calls an imaginary circle. I actually start looking through the lives of my church and people. When I look at people, I actually can see how this would apply to them. I start seeing a couple who just buried their 21-year-old son; or someone who just experienced a divorce, lost a job; their health has gone bad. I start looking at that and ask, "How does this passage apply?" Instead of me using nebulous terms such as "everybody has storms in life," I will say: "We know something about the storms of difficulty. Whether they are vocational, on our job, relationally with others, theologically with our faith, domestically within our home. . . . We have seen peaceful homes ripped apart by the winds of life. They've been ripped apart." I just start trying to name the storms

---

7   Bailey and Wiersbe, *Preaching in Black and White*, 88–90.
8   "Baylor University's Truett Seminary Announces 12 Most Effective Preachers in English-Speaking World," Baylor University, May 1, 2018, https://www.baylor.edu/mediacommunications/news.php?action=story&story=198528.

and really put a face and voice to what people are going through so they say, "Yeah, that's me."[9]

Dr. John Henry Williams, Jr. provides additional words of wisdom for sermon applications. With forty-plus years of pastoral ministry experience, Dr. Williams is an assistant professor of religion at Selma University and the former instructor of homiletics at Birmingham-Easonian Baptist Bible College. As a fourth-generation Black Baptist preacher, Dr. Williams writes about his preaching lineage in the forthcoming book *Three Days Journey into the Wilderness: A Story of Baptists in America.*

In conversations with Dr. Williams, he shared the following thoughts with the author:

> Traditional expository preaching presents a neat sermonic discourse on Sunday morning. However, a life-changing sermon may have jagged edges. These edges may cut the soul and stir spiritual conflict within the hearers. The cutting and conflict leads to a personal application of the sermon for the congregation. The preacher challenges the congregation to change their lives based on a biblical standard instead of conforming to a secular standard. Therefore, the test of a sermon's veracity is the outcome or effectiveness of its application in the life of the congregation.[10]

Sermon structure is vital for preaching a life-changing sermon. After studying the Scripture, it is important you organize your exegesis and thoughts so you can communicate your biblical message effectively.

---

9   Michal Duduit, "Preaching beyond the Walls: An Interview with Ralph Douglass West," *Preaching,* accessed February 3, 2021, https://www.preaching.com/articles/preaching-beyond-the-walls-an-interview-with-ralph-douglas-west.

10 Jesse Lawrence Nelson, "Equipping Selected Ministers of Macedonia Missionary Baptist Church, Panama City, Florida, with Essential Expository Preaching Skills" (DMin diss., New Orleans Baptist Theological Seminary, 2018), 15–16.

CHAPTER 5

SPEAKING IN THE SPIRIT

Have you been to Flunkersville? I had been preaching almost nine years before I visited this infamous place. I have not visited it often; however, I have traveled to it a few times. What is Flunkersville? Reverend Eddie Thomas, a senior statesman from South Alabama, was the first person I heard use the term. Flunkersville is the place the preacher goes when the sermons feels like it doesn't connect with the audience.

I remember my first trip to Flunkersville. I was pastoring my first church and preaching through the Sermon on the Mount. I completed a Greek exegesis course on the Sermon on the Mount the previous semester. The passage was Matthew 6:22–23. I explained the important words and used a couple of illustrations, but it still seemed as if I did not connect with the audience. The audience was silent. People were just staring at me. And if you have ever preached at a black church in the city with a rural and traditional culture, then you know that normally they will talk back to you. After the message, people just left. I stood in a somber spirit in the sanctuary. I knew I had been to Flunkersville. But I did not know why. Later, I realized: I was not speaking in the Spirit.

The fifth essential expository preaching skill is *speaking in the Spirit*. In order to be a life-changing preacher, you must deliver your message in the power of the Holy Spirit. In this chapter, I will discuss the anointing for preaching and give practical advice for sermon delivery.

WHAT IS THE ANOINTING?

In the Old Testament, anointing was an act of God that bestowed divine favor on the anointed person. Anointing was also associated with the outpouring of God's Spirit on the anointed person.[1] The Hebrew word for "anoint" is *masah*. It means "to smear or rub." The idea was to consecrate a person or object for service by rubbing with a liquid.[2] Priests, kings, and prophets were anointed for service. Moses anointed Aaron and his son as priests (Exod. 28:41). Samuel anointed Saul king of Israel (1 Sam. 9:16). After Saul disobeyed Yahweh, Samuel was directed to anoint David as the next king of Israel (1 Sam. 16:3, 12). Zadok the priest anointed Solomon as king of Israel (1 Kings 1:39). Isaiah said he was anointed by the Lord (Isa. 61:1).

In addition to being anointed with oil, these men were anointed by God's Spirit. Saul received the Spirit after Samuel anointed him. First Samuel 10:9–11 reads,

> Then it happened when he turned his back to leave Samuel, God changed his heart; and all those signs came about on that day. When they came to the hill there, behold, a group of prophets met him; and the Spirit of God came upon him mightily, so that he prophesied among them. It came about, when all who knew him previously saw that he prophesied now with the prophets, that the people said to one another, "What has happened to the son of Kish? Is Saul also among the prophets?"

The Spirit of God came upon David when he was anointed king. First Samuel 16:13 reads, "So Samuel took the horn of oil and anointed him in the midst of his brothers; and the Spirit of the Lord

---

1   J. A. Motyer, "Anointing, Anointed," *New Bible Dictionary*, eds. D. R. W. Wood, et al. (Downers Grove, IL: InterVarsity, 1996), 49.

2   James Swanson, *Dictionary of Biblical Languages with Semantic Domains: Hebrew (Old Testament)* (Oak Harbor, WA: Logos, 1997).

rushed upon David from that day forward. And Samuel set out and went to Ramah." The Spirit of the Lord was upon Isaiah the prophet. Isaiah 61:1–2 reads, "The Spirit of the Lord GOD is upon me, because the Lord anointed me to bring good news to the humble; he has sent me to bind up the brokenhearted, to proclaim release to captives and freedom to prisoners; to proclaim the favorable year of the LORD and the day of vengeance of our God; to comfort all who mourn." The Hebrew word for "came upon" is *salah*. This word means "to come in power" or "be forceful." This word conveys the idea of an overpowering force coupling with a lesser or more common force. The resulting actions are usually the will of the overpowering force.[3] The Holy Spirit came upon Saul and David and empowered them for leadership. The Holy Spirit came upon Isaiah and empowered him to prophesy.

In the New Testament the Greek word for "anoint" is *chrio*. This word means "to assign or appoint a person to a task."[4] In Luke 4:18–19, Jesus said the Spirit anointed him. The Scripture reads, "The Spirit of the Lord is upon me, because he anointed me to preach the gospel to the poor. He has sent me to proclaim release to the captives, and recovery of sight to the blind, to set free those who are oppressed, to proclaim the favorable year of the Lord."

When Jesus recited Isaiah 61:1–2 in Luke 4:18–19, he may not have been identifying himself as the Messiah. Instead, he could have been denoting the fact that he was fulfilling the role of a prophet because in Isaiah 61, the anointing is referring to a prophet, not Messiah.[5] As a prophet, Isaiah said he was anointed by God's Spirit to deliver the good news. Jesus said the Spirit anointed him to preach. Jesus preaching the gospel under the Spirit's anointing would help those who were dependent on God, release captives, give sight to the blind, liberate the oppressed, and usher in God's kingdom.[6]

---

3   Swanson, *Dictionary of Biblical Languages*.
4   Swanson, *Dictionary of Biblical Languages*.
5   I. Howard Marshall, *The Gospel of Luke: A Commentary on the Greek Text*, New International Greek Testament Commentary (Exeter: Paternoster, 1978), 183–84.
6   Marshall, *Gospel of Luke*.

In 1 John 2:20 and 27, the Greek word *chrisma* is used for "anoint." Like *chrio*, this word means "assignment for a particular task."[7] We know the initial readers of John's letters were Christians; however, the reference to the anointing could suggest the readers were church leaders. Just like prophets, priests, and kings, these church leaders were anointed for their position. Though this anointing could refer to all Christians, this idea is rare in the New Testament. John wanted to affirm the leaders' competency and assure them of their authority over false teachers and preachers.[8]

What does the anointing mean today? For preachers today, the anointing is the Spirit filling ministers to empower them for completing a specific task, like preaching. The Spirit controls the anointed preacher's thoughts, words, and actions. When preachers are under the anointing, they are not preaching. The Spirit is preaching through them.[9]

HOW DO PREACHERS BECOME ANOINTED?

In order to preach under the anointing, you must meet the following requirements. First, you must live a holy life. The Spirit cannot anoint ministers with sin abiding in their life. They must confess and repent of their sin. Second, you must live a prayerful life. Prayer demonstrates your desire for God. You should pray for your message to be simple and clear, so the people can understand God's Word and grow up in Christ. Third, you must live a surrendered life. You have to yield your will to God's will. You should pray "not my will but your will be done." Fourth, you must live a weak life. For example, the apostle Paul boasts about his weakness in 2 Corinthians 12:9–10 (NIV), "But he [God] said to me, 'My grace is sufficient for you, for my power is made perfect in weakness.' Therefore I will boast all the more gladly about my weaknesses, so that Christ's power may rest on me. That is why, for Christ's sake, I delight in weaknesses, in insults,

---

7   Swanson, *Dictionary of Biblical Languages.*
8   Zane C. Hodges, "1 John," in *The Bible Knowledge Commentary: An Exposition of the Scriptures*, eds. J. F. Walvoord and R. B. Zuck, vol. 2, *New Testament* (Wheaton, IL: Victor, 1985), 882.
9   Nelson, "Equipping," 51.

in hardships, in persecutions, in difficulties. For when I am weak, then I am strong."

The weakness Paul referenced was not a physical weakness, but a spiritual weakness. This weakness demonstrates your dependence on God instead dependence on your strength and gifts.

Fifth, you must live a humble life. You cannot be prideful in your gifts, abilities, or knowledge. So living a holy, prayerful, surrendered, weak, and humble life positions a minister the anointing of preaching.[10]

WHAT ARE THE RESULTS OF ANOINTED PREACHING?

According to James Earl Massey, an anointed preacher has a keen awareness of God's presence. The preacher has a sense of *kairos*, a special, opportune moment.[11] For Douglas Bennett, anointed preaching glorifies God, captivates the audience, and edifies Christians. Anointed preaching characterized the preaching of John the Baptist, Peter, Paul, and Jesus.[12]

David Martyn Lloyd-Jones says this about being anointed as you preach:

> It gives clarity of thought, clarity of speech, ease of utterance, a great sense of authority and confidence as you are preaching, an awareness of a power not your own thrilling through the whole of your being, and an indescribable sense of joy. You are a man "possessed," you are taken hold of, and taken up. I like to put it like this—and I know of nothing on earth that is comparable to this feeling—that when this happens you have a feeling that you are not

---

10   Nelson, "Equipping," 51.
11   Kevin W. Mannoia and Don Thorsen, *The Holiness Manifesto* (Grand Rapids: Eerdmans, 2008), 223.
12   Douglas Bennett, "Spirit-Anointed Preaching," Preaching.com, accessed September 3, 2019, https://www.preaching.com/articles/spirit-anointed-preaching.

actually doing the preaching, you are looking on at yourself in amazement as this is happening. It is not your effort; you are just the instrument, the channel, the vehicle: the Spirit is using you, and you are looking on in great enjoyment and astonishment.[13]

I noted several characteristics of anointed preaching in Greg Heisler's book *Spirit-Led Preaching*. First, the anointed preacher has boldness to speak the truth in love. Second, the anointing gives the minister freedom during the preaching moment. Third, the anointed preacher has vitality, which means the message is alive and full of life. Fourth, the anointing gives preachers power and insight beyond their human abilities or talents. Fifth, the Holy Spirit, who takes control of the preacher's delivery, possesses the anointed preacher.[14]

WHAT PREVENTS THE ANOINTING IN THE PREACHER'S LIFE?

Greg Heisler points out eight hindrances to anointed preaching:

* prayerlessness
* fear of man
* pride
* sin
* impure motives
* lack of preparation
* lack of belief
* lack of preaching Jesus[15]

How do ministers overcome these hindrances? If you desire the anointing, you must pray. Preachers who do not pray are powerless

---

13 David Martyn Lloyd-Jones, *Preaching and Preachers: The Classic Text with Essays from Mark Dever, Kevin DeYoung, Timothy Keller, John Piper, and Others* (Grand Rapids: Zondervan, 2011), 324.

14 Greg Heisler, *Spirit-Led Preaching* (Nashville: B&H, 2007), 136–40.

15 Heisler, *Spirit-Led Preaching*, 127.

preachers. No prayer means no power, but much prayer equals much power for preaching. You cannot be fearful of people. Preachers who fear people should remind themselves of God's words to Jeremiah the prophet: "Do not be afraid of them, for I am with you to save you. . . . Behold, I have put My words in your mouth. See, I have appointed you this day over the nations and over the kingdoms, to pluck up and to break down, to destroy and to overthrow, to build and to plant" (Jer. 1:8–10).

To be an anointed preacher, you must fight your pride with humility because God gives grace to the humble. You must rid yourself of sin because you are called to holiness. You must be aware of your motives. You can ask for the anointing, but you will not receive it if your motives are not pure. You must study God's Word so you will be approved by God and accurately interpret God's Word. You must walk by faith and not just human intellect. You must believe in the provision of God, the person of Jesus Christ, and the power of the Holy Spirit for anointed preaching. You must preach Christ Jesus and him crucified.

HOW DO I DELIVER A SPIRIT-FILLED SERMON?

As I reflect on preaching a Spirit-filled sermon, four words come to mind: passion, pace, practice, and preparation. We should deliver our sermons with passion. This passion is not self-generated. Passion comes from time with God in personal worship, Bible study, and prayer.

Passion grows from being filled with the Spirit. Being Spirit-filled is like A, B, C: *asking, believing,* and *complying* are requirements for being filled with the Spirit. First, you must pour yourself out in prayer and ask the Holy Spirit to fill you up. Second, you must believe you are filled with the Spirit. One can be filled with the Spirit and not feel the Spirit. Third, you must comply with the Spirit's leadership for life and ministry.

My passion for preaching grows from meditating on the preaching text. My passion grows from thinking about the joy of preaching. I believe you can also grow your passion by envisioning yourself delivering the sermon to the people. God chose you to be his spokesperson for the gospel—the gospel preached that liberates people from sin, the gospel applied that helps people live a sanctified life.

In addition to passion, we must watch our pace. Sometimes our passion can speed up our preaching pace. You can lose the people if you go too fast. You should develop a moderate pace and a steady rhythm. How do we find our pace? This leads to my next thought for sermon delivery.

Practice, practice, practice! Yes! Practice your preaching. Practicing your preaching is not an unspiritual practice. It's part of the preparation. When I first started preaching, I would practice the whole sermon in front of the mirror. In my first pastorate, I would practice my sermon during the commute to church. Now, I may just practice my introduction and transition into my first point.

Some preachers prefer to preach from a full manuscript. Others prefer an outline or a few notes. I know a few preachers who write a full manuscript and preach it from memory. What you decide to do might change from one sermon to the next.

I preach from a full manuscript when I want to be particular about my word choice throughout the sermon and avoid catch phrases. I use a full outline when I want to mention specific details. The full outline will resemble the sermon outline you learned to construct in chapter 4. However, I include more details in the explanation, illustration, and application of the sermon.

Oftentimes, I preach extemporaneously. I will take a basic outline to the pulpit. I will include my MPT, LCP, sermon points, application notes, and a few notes on the conclusion. I usually write this on a half-sheet so it will fit in my Bible. I have also written notes on post it notes. At times, I have had to do an impromptu sermon, which is a sermon with no prior preparation. I have had to preach impromptu sermons at conferences, funerals, and other church events. Before preaching, I pray, select a text, develop a short outline, and preach.

AN ANOINTED PREACHER

Dr. Robert Smith Jr. is an anointed preacher. He currently occupies the Charles T. Carter Baptist Chair of Divinity at Beeson

Divinity School where he has taught Christian preaching since 1997. He authored *Doctrine That Dances: Bringing Doctrinal Preaching and Teaching to Life*, which received the 2008 Preaching Book of the Year Award by *Preaching* magazine and the 2009 Preaching Book of the Year Award by *Christianity Today's* Preaching.com. The book was named one of the twenty-five most influential preaching books in the last twenty-five years by *Preaching* magazine in 2010. Smith was the recipient of the 2017 E. K. and V. M. Bailey Living Legend Award.[16]

In *Doctrine That Dances*, Dr. Smith gives the reader a primer for sermon delivery. Step 1 is "identification—start low." This step involves the preparation of the sermon and the preacher. Preachers must prepare their mind, body, and spirit. Smith challenges his students to read the passage fifty times before studying it so they can feel the text with all of their senses.

Step 2 is "clarification—go slow." Preachers may become exhausted if they begin the sermon too rapidly. The listeners may lose interest if they cannot keep up with the preacher's pace. Ministers must also know the direction they are headed in the sermon. Knowing how the sermon will end is as important as knowing how it will begin.

Step 3 is "intensification—rise." The sermon moves through the rising emotions of the preacher as the preacher explains the text in the power of the Spirit. The intensity of emotions will rise as the minister exalts God through Christ. The preacher should not be afraid of the emotions that are stirred up.

Step 4 is "application—strike fire." The preacher desires for the audience to experience the meaning, the purpose, and the message. Smith notes that meaning and application are weaknesses in modern preaching. No text can mean in the present what it did not mean in the past.

Step 5 is "recapitulation—retire." In coming down, the minister must trust God to move in the life of the audience. Retiring refers to the sermon's conclusion. After flying high, the preacher must prepare to land.

---

16 Nelson, "Equipping," 154–55.

Step 6 is "motivation—sit down in a storm." As the preacher sits down, the people are getting up. They are getting up to do the work of ministry. They are getting up to apply the expounded truth in their lives. They are getting up to go and tell others what has lit them on fire from the Word.[17]

WORDS OF WISDOM

Dr. Greg Heisler is pastor of Madison Avenue Baptist Church in Maryville, Tennessee, author of *Spirit-Led Preaching*, and former professor of expository preaching at Southeastern Baptist Theological Seminary. Here are his wise words on speaking in the Spirit:

> If the preacher's life is not characterized by love, joy, peace, patience, kindness, goodness, gentleness, faithfulness, and self-control, then his preaching will not be characterized by the Spirit's power. The Spirit must first mark the preacher's life before he marks his preaching. The fruit of the Holy Spirit in our lives gives birth to the power of the Holy Spirit in our preaching.[18]

Do you speak in the Spirit? It is impossible to speak in the Spirit without the anointing. Preaching under the anointing requires you to live a holy life, prayerful life, surrendered life, weak life, and a humble life. When you are anointed, the Spirit is speaking through you to change the lives of your audience. So the anointing is essential for preaching life-changing sermons.

---

17 Robert Smith, *Doctrine That Dances: Bringing Doctrinal Preaching and Teaching to Life* (Nashville: B&H Academic, 2008), 42–44.
18 Heisler, *Spirit-Led Preaching*, 132.

CHAPTER 6

SHARING THE SAVIOR

I preached the gospel every Sunday. I was taught that a sermon was not complete without going by the cross. This means I had to include the birth, life, death, burial, and resurrection of Jesus Christ in every sermon. Often times the "cross moment" came after my conclusion. I would find a way to creatively transition from my conclusion to my invitation. I would preach Jesus. But then one day I realized that although I preached the gospel, I was not explaining the gospel. I would preach the gospel—the birth, life, death, and resurrection of Jesus Christ every Sunday. However, it was more of a *celebration* of the gospel than an *explanation* of the gospel. I told people he was born, he lived, he died, and rose again, but I failed to tell them why he was born, the purpose of his life, why he died, and the significance of his resurrection. So when I invited people to come to the altar and surrender their life to Christ, sometimes I would get blank stares because I was preaching the gospel and not explaining the gospel during my invitation.

How do you share a gospel invitation? The sixth essential expository preaching skill is *sharing the Savior*.

HOW TO GIVE A GOSPEL INVITATION

On the road to Emmaus, Jesus explained the things concerning himself in all the Scriptures, beginning with Moses and all the prophets (Luke 24:27). Expository preaching is Christ-centered. You must share Jesus. "Christ-centered" does not mean we bend every Scripture toward Christ. Instead, we reveal Christ in the Scripture. Every Scripture is not typological but an example of Christ's character. You can share Jesus in the sermon through an explanation, illustration, or application of how the text connects to Christ. The preacher can share Jesus after the sermon with an invitation. When giving a gospel invitation, you should intentionally transition from the conclusion to the invitation, just as you use transitions within the sermon as you go from one sermon point to the next. You don't want to conclude a message and then abruptly offer the invitation.

During the invitation, you should clarify what you want the audience to do in response to the invitation. Do you want them to believe? Do you want them to close their eyes and bow their head and say a prayer? Maybe you want them to walk the aisle, come to the altar, or meet with a prayer leader. You might tell them to talk with someone after the invitation and conclusion of the service.

Sometimes I have asked people to walk the aisle. Other times I directed people to talk with me or another minister after the church service. After the invitation I may ask everyone to close their eyes and raise their hands if they desire to surrender their life to Jesus. Then I may ask them all to pray for repentance and salvation for the forgiveness of sins. I ask the entire congregation to repeat after me and say,

> Dear Heavenly Father, have mercy on me and forgive me for my sins. Thank you for your son Jesus Christ and the death he died because of my sins. I repent of my sins and surrender my life. I believe that he died for my sins, and I surrender my life to him today. Now fill me with your Holy Spirit and help me walk in obedience. In Jesus's name, amen.

I assure them the act of prayer does not save them. Their faith in Jesus Christ is the basis of their salvation.

AN INVITATION THAT CONNECTS WITH THE SERMON

The following invitation is one I used after concluding a message on 1 Corinthians 13:1–7. The invitation connects with the actual sermon topic.

Love: you can live with it, but you cannot live without it. If it was not for love, God's love, I would be spiritually dead. I thank God for his love because "God shows his love for us in that while we were still sinners Christ died for us" (Rom. 5:8 RSV). Yes, we are sinners. The Bible reads, "All have sinned and fall short of God's glory" (Rom. 3:23 CEB). Do you know what the reward is for sin? Death! The Bible reads, "The wages of sin is death" (Rom. 6:23). But the good news is that because of God's love for us, we don't have to die. We can have eternal life: "For God so loved the world that he gave his one and only Son. Anyone who believes in [his Son Jesus Christ] will not die but will have eternal life" (John 3:16 NIRV). Do you want to believe in Christ today? Do you want to learn more about Jesus Christ and how to have a relationship with him? Come and meet me at the altar, so we can talk about you and him.

PERSONAL TESTIMONY AS AN INVITATION

I have used my personal testimony as an invitation when I want to connect with the audience in a personal way. I did not have a relationship with God before I became a Christian. I was committed to going to church, but I was not committed to God. I would lie, steal, and disobey my parents. My relationship with God began one evening when watching Dr. Charles F. Stanley on *In Touch*. He proclaimed the gospel at the end of his sermon. I realized four things after hearing the gospel: 1) I was a sinner; 2) the wages of sin is death; 3) I needed a Savior; 4) Jesus Christ (the Savior) died for my sins and rose from the dead. So that evening I repented of my sins, and I believed in Christ as my Savior. I asked God to forgive me for my sins, and I surrendered my life to him. When I became a Christian, I felt like a new person. The Bible says, "Therefore if any man be in Christ, he is a new creature: old things are passed away; behold, new things have come" (2 Cor. 5:17). My whole life changed. I committed my life to Christ and his church. I desired God and godly things. I had more than religion; I had a relationship with God. I read the Bible everyday and communicated with God through prayer and worship. I was not satisfied with being good. I wanted to be like Jesus Christ; I wanted to be holy. That's my testimony: the story of how I became a Christian. Do you want to become a Christian? It is simple! Turn away from your sins and trust in Jesus to save you from your sins!

A GOSPEL PREACHER

Reverend Dr. Marcus Demond Davidson is the senior pastor of New Mount Olive Baptist Church in Fort Lauderdale, Florida, and president and CEO of PMD Ministries, which offers seminars, lectures, workshops, and curricula focusing on leadership. He is the coauthor of *The Power of Leadership* with Frank Kennedy Jr.

Rev. Davidson is a graduate (BA) of Alabama Agricultural and Mechanical University (a historic black college and university in Normal, Alabama), Heritage Bible College (MABS), Beeson Divinity School (MDiv), and the Southern Baptist Theological Seminary (DMin). He currently serves as the president of the Youth and Young Adult Auxiliary of the National Baptist Convention, USA.[1]

In addition to his pastoral preaching, Dr. Davidson travels nationally and internationally, preaching the gospel of Jesus Christ to thousands of souls. So what is Dr. Davidson's philosophy on sharing the Savior?

There are many important aspects to a sermon such as the introduction, the body, illustrations, culture, context, exposition, application, eye contact, vocal intonation, clarity of speech, and the list could go on. Nonetheless, there is another facet to the sermon that is of paramount importance, and it is the invitation to receive Jesus as Lord and Savior. Giving the invitation is not a trivial matter and should not be casually presented. Therefore, it should be part of the sermonic preparation so that it can be carefully presented.

To effectively share the Savior invitationally during the sermon, one should see sharing Jesus as the ultimate destination in the

---

1   "Our Pastor," New Mount Olive Baptist Church, accessed January 29, 2021, http://mountolive.org/ourpastor.

sermonic journey. Just as in music there is what is known as the crescendo—the song builds to that majestic moment—so with the sermon: it should build to the moment of sharing Jesus. Once one gets to this moment, sharing the Savior should be done substantively, with clarity, and passionately. The listener should not feel as though he or she is being coerced but compelled. I simply call it the "joy moment," the moment when someone is on the precipice of experiencing the unspeakable joy of knowing Jesus as Lord and Savior of their life.[2]

WORDS OF WISDOM

Dr. Preston Nix is Professor of Evangelism and Evangelistic Preaching, occupying the Roland Q. Leavell Chairman of Evangelism, and chairman of the Pastoral Ministries Division at New Orleans Baptist Theological Seminary. He shares words of wisdom from nearly fifty years of experience in evangelistic ministry:

> The ultimate life change occurs when a person gives his heart to Christ and is born again. As a result, whenever a biblical, life-changing sermon is preached, the preacher always should share the Gospel at the conclusion of the message admonishing the listeners to repent of their sin and to trust Jesus as their Savior and Lord. Because all of Scripture bears witness of Christ, whatever the text of the sermon, the message should culminate in a Gospel invitation for the listeners to place their faith in the Lord Jesus Christ and be saved. The Gospel invitation must be given clearly, thoroughly, authoritatively, urgently, passionately, persuasively, smoothly, and expectantly. Most importantly, the Gospel invitation must be extended with total dependency upon the Holy Spirit. Only the Holy Spirit can bring about conviction of sin and conversion of the soul. The Gospel invitation can be extended by means

---

2   Marcus Davidson, email message to the author, January 27, 2021. Used by permission.

of personal prayer for salvation, an altar call, a counseling room, a response card, raised hands, eye contact, a personal meeting, or a multiple approach employing two or more of the aforementioned methods. Whatever the method or methods employed, a biblical, life-changing sermon always should conclude with a Gospel invitation giving the listeners an opportunity to decide for Christ and experience the ultimate life change![3]

How do you share the Savior? The ultimate life change in a life-changing sermon is when the listeners surrender their lives to Jesus Christ, our Lord and Savior. We cannot save people, but we can share the Savior. It is important that you share the Savior so that lost souls can be saved.

---

3   Preston Nix, email message to the author, January 30, 2021. Used by permission.

CONCLUSION

What kind of sermon will your audience hear the next time you preach? Will they hear an informational sermon? A sermon filled with facts and statistics from a Google search? Maybe they will they hear an inspirational sermon, a sermon preached to uplift their spirit. Or they might hear an instructional sermon, a sermon designed to teach how to fix a problem in their life.

Whatever they hear, your audience needs more than an informational, inspirational, or instructional sermon. People need to hear a life-changing sermon. A sermon that is biblical, theological, Christ-centered, Spirit-filled, and practical. Preach a sermon that people can see, feel, and do. Preach a sermon that will place God's Word into people's heads, hearts, and hands. Preach a sermon that will inform people of God's will and instruct them in the way of the Spirit. Preach a sermon that will encourage people to look, live, and love like Jesus Christ. Preach a life-changing sermon.

How do you preach life-changing sermons? I hope you have found that answer in this book. Preaching life-changing sermons begins with you seeking the Spirit. This requires you to spend extensive time in prayer. The power of preachers is in their praying, not their preaching. After seeking the Spirit, you will select the Scripture. You must ask God what he wants you to say to his people. This may be a short series on a topic or a series on a passage or a whole book. Once you select the Scripture, you have to study the Scripture by asking three big questions. What does the text say, what does the text mean, and how does the text apply to our lives? After answering those questions, you should structure the sermon. You can vary the structures of your sermons, which promotes creativity and freshness. No matter how creative your structure, you will need to be filled with the Spirit so that you can speak in the Spirit. It is impossible to preach life-changing sermons without the power of the Holy Spirit. Like the Holy Spirit, you will testify about Jesus as you share the Savior. Life change begins with Jesus and is the crucible of life-changing preaching!

Now that you know how to preach life-changing sermons, you have to decide if you will be a life-changing preacher. It is not easy preaching biblical sermons. Sometimes you may be tempted to deviate from developing and delivering biblical sermons because these sermons are not always popular. However, a life-changing preacher does not preach for the popularity, a life-changing preacher preaches for the pleasure of God. If you ever get tired of preaching biblical sermons, remember Paul's final words to Timothy:

> I solemnly charge you in the presence of God and of Christ Jesus, who is to judge the living and the dead, and by His appearing and His kingdom: preach the word; be ready in season and out of season; reprove, rebuke, exhort, with great patience and instruction. For the time will come when they will not endure sound doctrine; but wanting to have their ears tickled, they will accumulate for themselves teachers in accordance to their own desires, and will turn away their ears from the truth and will turn aside to myths. But you, be sober in all things, endure hardship, do the work of an evangelist, fulfill your ministry. (2 Tim. 4:1–5, NASB 1995)

LIFE-CHANGING SERMON GUIDE

Y ou can complete this life-changing sermon guide in one day or five days. If your primary day for preaching is Sunday, I suggest you start working on this sermon guide on Monday and complete it by Friday. This schedule will allow you to rest, reflect, or complete your sermon on Saturday and review it sermon on Sunday.

LIFE-CHANGING SERMON GUIDE

Seeking the Spirit and Selecting the Scripture (Monday)

1. What does God want to say to the people?

Meditate on three questions:

- Who does God want the people to be?
- What does God want the people to do?
- What does God want the people to know?

2. What do the people need to hear from God? I pray through this question too.

- How do the people need to grow in Christ?
- What sins do the people need to stop? Of course people need

to stop all forms of sin, but I am asking which sins are most prevalent in their lives.
- What doctrine needs to be taught?
- What spiritual discipline needs to be emphasized, like prayer, evangelism, stewardship, or worship?
- What Bible book will parallel with the church in this season of ministry and the people's lives?

Studying the Scripture (Tuesday)

Pray

- Ask the Spirit to open your eyes so you can see the truth of the Scriptures (Ps. 119:18).
- Ask the Spirit to guide your during the process of studying the text.
- Thank the Spirit for the insight and understanding you receive while studying the text.

Historical Background Study

Answer in complete sentences. Provide as much detail as possible.

1. Who is the author of the book?
2. Who are the recipients of the book?
3. When was the book written?
4. Where was the author when he wrote the book?
5. What occasion or events caused the author to write the book?
6. What is the purpose of the book? Why was it written?
7. What is the book's literary genre?
8. Where is this book in biblical and world history?
9. What were the social and cultural norms of the recipients?
10. What was the recipients' understanding of God?

Studying the Scripture (Wednesday)

Observation—What Does It Say? (Six Clues)

1. What is emphasized?
2. What is repeated?
3. What is related?
4. What is alike?
5. What is unalike?
6. What is true to life?

Observation—What Does It Say? (Six Questions)

1. Who?
2. What?
3. When?
4. Where?
5. Why?
6. How?

Interpretation—What Does It Mean?

1. Content:
2. Context:
3. Comparison:
4. Culture:
5. Consultation:

Application—How Does the Text Apply to My Life?

1. Forgiveness—Do you have any sins to confess?
2. Attitude and Actions—How will you try to change?
3. Insight and Instruction—What did you learn from today's Scripture reading?

4. Thanksgiving—Did you see any reason to praise God?
5. Helping Others—What did you see today that could encourage someone else?

Structuring the Sermon (Thursday)

Textual Outline

Scripture:

1. What is the subject?
2. What is the author saying about the subject?
3. What is the main point of the text (MPT)?

MPT:

Outline:

    I.

    II.

    III.

Structuring the Sermon (Friday)

Choose which sermon structure you will use and decide if you will preach from a full manuscript, from a detailed outline, from memory, or extemporaneously.

Sermon Outline

    Sermon Title:

    Text:

Subject:

MPT:

LCP:

POS:

KW:

TS:

Introduction

Sermon Points

  I.

    a.

    b.

  II.

    a.

    b.

  III.

    a.

    b.

Conclusion

Illustration ideas: stories, sports, songs, social media, etc.
(optional)

Application ideas: social, emotional, mental, spiritual, relational, financial, physical, etc. (optional)

Invitation ideas: sermon connection, personal testimony, Romans Road, etc.

Speaking in the Spirit and Sharing the Savior (Sunday)

EXAMPLE SERMON OUTLINES

UNDERSTANDING SPIRITUAL GIFTS, 1 CORINTHIANS 12–14

Sermon 1

Sermon Title: Gifts of the Spirit

Text: 1 Corinthians 12:1–11

Subject: Gifts

MPT: In 1 Corinthians 12:1–11, Paul informed the Corinthians about the gifts the Holy Spirit gave to the church.

LCP: The Spirit manifests gifts in Christians today, so we must be aware of the various spiritual gifts.

POS: Hearers will assess their spiritual gifts based on the gifts listed in the Scripture.

Introduction

In 1 Corinthians 12:1–11, Paul informed the Corinthians of the gifts the Holy Spirit gave to the church. The Spirit manifests gifts in Christians today, so we must be aware of the various spiritual gifts. Two questions come to mind when I read today's Scripture. Who gives the gifts to the church and what are the spiritual gifts in the church? The first question we want to answer is who gives the gifts?

Sermon Points
1. Who gives the gifts to the church (1 Cor. 12:1–7)?
2. What gifts does the Spirit give the church (1 Cor. 12:8–11)?

Conclusion
    After studying today's Scripture, we have observed Paul's who, what, and why regarding spiritual gifts. Paul knew it was important for the Corinthians to understand spiritual gifts, so he informed the Corinthians about the gifts the Holy Spirit gave to the church. The Spirit manifests gifts in Christians today, so we must be aware of the various spiritual gifts. Like the Corinthians, it is important for us to acknowledge and assess our gifts.

Illustration ideas: Tell a story about my daughter receiving gifts from Dollar Tree to illustrate the significance that gifts are based on the giver of the gift and not the gift itself.

Application ideas: Highlight the differences between spiritual gifts, natural gifts, talents, and skills.

Invitation ideas: Sermon connection—Without Christ it is impossible to receive the gift from the Spirit because Christ gives us the Spirit that provides the spiritual gift.

Sermon 2

Sermon Title: One Body

Text: 1 Corinthians 12:12–26

Subject: Unity

MPT: Paul explained how the Corinthians were one body in Christ and the significance of all body parts.

LCP: Every member of the church is vital because the church is one body in Christ.

POS: Hearers will remove walls that divide the church to become one body in Christ.

Introduction
How do you describe the church? Rick Warren calls the church a family. In today's Scripture, Paul referred to the church as a body. He explained how the Corinthians were one body in Christ and that each part of the body was important. So our church is a body with many parts. Every member of the church is vital because the church is one body in Christ. Let's notice the details of the text.

Sermon Points
1. We are one body with one Spirit (1 Cor. 12:12–14).
2. Every member is significant (1 Cor. 12:15–21).
3. Our affections must be the same (1 Cor. 12:22–26).

Conclusion
Rick Warren calls the church a family. I think the church is a team. And the apostle Paul referred to the church as a body. In the passage we studied today, Paul explained how the Corinthians were one body in Christ and that each part of the body was important. Our church is no different than the Corinthians. In order to remove the walls of separation, we must know that every member of the church is vital because the church is one body in Christ.

Illustration ideas: Use a team sport illustration to describe how the church has many members but one body.

Application ideas: Our significance is not based on where we are in the body but what we are doing in the body.

Invitation ideas: Sermon connection: Are you part of the body of Christ? Do you want to be a member of God's family? If you accept Jesus, he will bring you into the family of God (John 1:12).

Sermon 3

Sermon Title: Desire the Greater Gifts

Text: 1 Corinthians 12:27–31

Subject: Greater Gifts

MPT: Paul encouraged the Corinthians to pursue the greater gifts from the list he provided to them.

LCP: It is imperative to desire the greater gifts.

POS: Hearers will begin to pursue the greater gifts.

Introduction

What gifts do you desire? Do you want the gift of prophecy, administration, knowledge, or tongues? When we read today's Scripture, we notice that Paul encouraged the Corinthians to pursue the greater gifts from the list he provided to them. That Christians know their spiritual gifts is a big concern for the contemporary church. It is important for Christians to know their spiritual gifts, but it is imperative to desire the greater gifts. Now let's turn our attention to what the apostle Paul wrote to the Corinthians.

Sermon Points

1. God designates gifts in the church (1 Cor. 12:27–28).

2. We do not all have the same gifts (1 Cor. 12:9–30).
3. We must desire the greater gifts (1 Cor. 12:29–31).

Conclusion

What gifts do you desire? Paul encouraged the Corinthians to pursue the greater gifts from the list he provided to them. It is important for Christians to know their spiritual gifts, but it is imperative to desire the greater gifts. I hope you desire the greater gifts.

Illustration ideas: Use illustrations of people in history who pursued greatness like Martin Luther King Jr., Shirley Chisholm, and Tom Brady.

Application ideas: Emotions like fear and anxiety can cause us to settle for the good instead of pursing the great.

Invitation ideas: Personal testimony about good versus great with transition to the gospel.

Sermon 4

Sermon Title: The Necessity of Love

Text: 1 Corinthians 13:1–7

Subject: Love

MPT: Paul's exposition on love signified its importance as a required characteristic in the life of the Corinthians.

LCP: As Christians, we must realize that love is a necessary attribute in the Christian's life.

POS: Hearers will exhibit love toward one another.

Introduction

Do you have love? As Christians, do we need love? Paul will answer these questions for the Christian in the twenty-first century, just as he answered these questions for the Corinthian Christians in the first century. In our text today, we note that Paul's exposition on love signified its importance as a required characteristic in the life of the Corinthians. And because the word of God does not change, as stated by the prophet Isaiah, "The grass withers, the flower fades . . . but the word of our God stands forever" (Isa. 40:7–8), as Christians, we must realize that love is a necessary attribute in the Christian's life. Because love is necessary to walk in the more excellent way, you and I must have love. So why do we need love? Can't we live a Christian life that is satisfactory to God without having love? As we analyze this text, we will notice three truths that illustrate why Christians need love.

Sermon Points
1. Without love, our spiritual gifts are not effective (1 Cor. 13:1–3).
2. With love, our Christian character is exhibited (1 Cor. 13:4–6).
3. With love, we have endurance (1 Cor. 13:7).

Conclusion

Do you have love? Do you believe it has a vital role in our Christian lives? In our text we noted that Paul's exposition on love signified its importance as a required characteristic in the life of the Corinthians because it was the more excellent way. As Christians, we must realize that love is a necessary attribute in our lives, because love is necessary: God demonstrated it, Jesus commanded us to do it, the Holy Spirit reaches people through it, and Paul preached it. Therefore my desire is for you to possess it. You and I must have love. Without love our spiritual gifts are not effective. With love our Christian character is exhibited. And with love we are able to endure all temptation.

Illustration ideas: Reference song lyrics from *Love* by Musiq Soulchild.

Application ideas: social, emotional, mental, spiritual, relational, financial, physical, etc. (optional)

Invitation ideas: Sermon connection—Love: you can live with it, but you cannot live without it. If it was not for love, God's love, I would be spiritually dead. I thank God for his love because "God shows his love for us in that while we were still sinners, Christ died for us" (Rom. 5:8 ESV).

Sermon 5

Sermon Title: Love Is the Greatest Gift

Text: 1 Corinthians 13:8–13

Subject: The Greatest Gift

MPT: Paul told the Corinthians that love was the greatest of the three gifts that would remain.

LCP: Christians mistakenly prioritize the gifts of prophecy and tongues, but the Bible teaches us that love is the greatest gift.

POS: Hearers will prioritize love as the primary gift.

Introduction

If you could only choose one gift, which gift would you choose? Would you pick prophecy, tongues, or knowledge? The apostle Paul would choose love. Paul told the Corinthians that love was the greatest of the three gifts that would remain. Christians today are no different than the Corinthians. Christians mistakenly prioritize the gifts of prophecy and tongues, but the Bible teaches us that love is the greatest gift. So why is love the greatest gift?

Sermon Points
1. Love never fails (1 Cor. 13:8–10).
2. Love is greater than faith and hope (1 Cor. 13:13).

Conclusion
The apostle Paul would choose love. Paul told the Corinthians that love was the greatest of the three gifts that would remain. One day, prophecy, tongues, and knowledge will cease. Christians mistakenly prioritize the gifts of prophecy and tongues, but the Bible teaches us that love is the greatest gift. Do you have love?

Illustration ideas: Illustrate the difference between good versus great at home, work, school, and church.

Application ideas: It is good to be good, but it is better to be great.

Invitation ideas: John 3:16—the greatest demonstration of love.

Sermon 6

Sermon Title: Prophecy vs. Tongues—Part 1

Text: 1 Corinthians 14:1–19

Subject: Spiritual Gifts

MPT: Paul exhorted the Corinthians to seek the gift of prophecy because it profited the church more than tongues.

LCP: Between the gifts of tongues and prophecy, Christians should desire prophecy more than tongues because prophecy edifies the church.

POS: Hearers will pray for a heart that desires prophecy over tongues.

Introduction
   If you could choose between the gifts of prophecy or tongues, which gift would you choose? Paul exhorted the Corinthians to seek the gift of prophecy because it profited the church more than tongues. Between the gifts of tongues and prophecy, Christians should desire prophecy more than tongues because prophecy edifies the church. So why should Christians choose prophecy instead of tongues?

Sermon Points
1. What is the contrast with prophecy and tongues (1 Cor. 14:1–5)?
2. What was the conflict with tongues (1 Cor. 14:6–12)?
3. What are concerns with praying in tongues (1 Cor. 14:13–19)?

Conclusion
   Prophecy or tongues, which gift would you choose? Paul exhorted the Corinthians to seek the gift of prophecy because it profited the church more than tongues. Between the gifts of tongues and prophecy, Christians should desire prophecy more than tongues because prophecy edifies the church. Which gift would you choose?

Illustration ideas: Read from the Greek New Testament (pronouncing the words in Greek) to illustrate that no one will be edified by me reading in Greek unless they can interpret Greek.

Application ideas: "Don't be so heavenly minded that you are no earthly good."

Invitation ideas: Sermon connection—Jesus wants you to be edified so that he might be glorified through your life. Therefore, he kept the message of the gospel simple and clear, that is, believe and repent.

Sermon 7

Sermon Title: Prophecy vs. Tongues—Part 2

Text: 1 Corinthians 14:20–28

Subject: Spiritual Gifts

MPT: Paul continued his discourse on prophecy versus tongues by contrasting the gifts' benefits for believers and unbelievers.

LCP: We must distinguish between the purposes of prophecy and tongues so we can minister effectively to believers and unbelievers.

POS: Hearers will minister effectively to believers and unbelievers.

Introduction

Every Christian is given a gift, and every gift has a purpose. Paul continued his discourse on prophecy versus tongues by contrasting the gifts' benefits for believers and unbelievers. As discerning Christians, we must distinguish between the purposes of prophecy and tongues so we can minister effectively to believers and unbelievers. So how does prophecy differ from tongues?

Sermon Points

1. We must clarify the roles of prophecy and tongues (1 Cor. 14:20–22).
2. We cannot ignore the confusion tongues can cause (1 Cor. 14:23).
3. We will glorify God through the conviction of prophecy (1 Cor. 14: 24–25).

Conclusion

Do you know the difference between prophecy and tongues? Paul continued his discourse on prophecy versus tongues by contrasting the gifts' benefits for believers and unbelievers. As discerning Christians, we must distinguish between the purposes of prophecy and tongues so we can minister effectively to believers and unbelievers. How effective is your ministry?

Illustration ideas: A story to illustrate that negative results of not using an object for its intended purpose.

Application ideas: Knowing when to do something is just as important as knowing how to do something.

Invitation ideas: Sermon connection: Jesus wants you to know and understand the gospel. Therefore, he kept the message of the gospel simple and clear—that is, believe and repent.

Sermon 8

Sermon Title: The Order of Things

Text: 1 Corinthians 14:26–40

MPT: Paul concluded his discourse on spiritual gifts by instructing the Corinthians to do all things in an orderly manner.

LCP: The church has numerous gifts working through various personalities; therefore, everything must be done in order.

POS: Hearers will submit to the order of things in the church.

Introduction
God is not a God of confusion but peace. Peace is absent from churches that lack order. Paul concluded his discourse on spiritual gifts by instructing the Corinthians to do all things in an orderly manner. The church has numerous gifts working through various personalities; therefore, everything must be done in order. So what does this say about order?

Sermon Points
1. The Bible gives us directions for the assembly (1 Cor. 14:26–33).
2. The Bible gives us directions for women (1 Cor. 14:34–36).
3. The Bible gives us directions for tongues and prophecy (1 Cor. 14:37–40).

Conclusion

Paul concluded his discourse on spiritual gifts by instructing the Corinthians to do all things in an orderly manner. The church has numerous gifts working through various personalities; therefore, everything must be done in order. Would you describe our church as one that does all things properly and in order?

Illustration ideas: Tell a story about the history of Robert's Rules of Order

Application ideas: Chaos will reign where order does not rule.

Invitation ideas: Is your life chaotic? Jesus did all things well (Mark 7:37) and in an orderly. Bringing Jesus into your life and letting him rule your life will bring order to your life.

EXAMPLE SERMONS

I n this section, I have included an example for each of the five sermon structures I referred to in chapter 4: that is, rhetorical, question-answer, then-now, key word, and devotional. The first three sermons are complete word-for-word manuscripts and the last two sermons are outlines of the sermon.

A RHETORICAL SERMON:
THE NECESSITY OF LOVE (1 COR. 13:1–7)

Text

If I speak with the tongues of men and of angels, but do not have love, I have become a noisy gong or a clanging cymbal. If I have the gift of prophecy, and know all mysteries and all knowledge; and if I have all faith, so as to remove mountains, but do not have love, I am nothing. And if I give all my possessions to feed the poor, and if I surrender my body to be burned, but do not have love, it profits me nothing. Love is patient, love is kind and is not jealous; love does not brag and is not arrogant, does not act unbecomingly; it does not seek its own, is not provoked, does not take into account a wrong suffered, does not rejoice in unrighteousness, but rejoices with the truth; bears all things, believes all things, hopes all things, endures all things. (1 Cor. 13:1–7 NASB 1995)

Introduction

Do you have love? As Christians, do we need love? Paul will answer these questions for the Christian in the twenty-first century, just as he answered these questions for the Corinthian Christians in the first century. In our text today, we note that Paul's exposition on love signified its importance as a required characteristic in the life of the Corinthians. And because the word of God does not change, as stated by the prophet Isaiah, "The grass withers, the flower fades, . . . but the word of our God stands forever" (Isa. 40:7–9), we must realize that as followers of Christ, love is a necessary attribute in the Christian's life. Because love is necessary to walk in the more excellent way, you and I must have love. So why do we need love? Can't we live a Christian life that is satisfactory to God without having love? As we analyze this text, we will notice three truths that illustrate why Christians need love.

Sermon Points

Truth 1—Without love, our spiritual gifts are not effective (vv. 1–3).

After reading these verses, we notice that Paul told the Corinthians that love was necessary in order for one to use spiritual gifts effectively. Paul was saying that if he spoke in the tongues of humans or angels—literally a heavenly language—but did not have love, then his speaking in tongues would become a booming gong or crashing cymbal. He told the Corinthians that without love, his possession of the spiritual gifts of prophecy, knowledge, and faith were meaningless. Paul went on to say that if he could possibly give away his possessions piece by piece (also translated as "bit by bit" or "to dole out") but did not it do it with love, then he would benefit nothing. So if the Corinthian church were to auction off all of their possessions without receiving any compensation but had no love, they would benefit nothing. Consequently, their almsgiving would be in vain. Many of our churches are dying, slowly but surely. Notice I said *our* churches, not Christ's church. They are not dying because of lacking spiritual gifts. The twenty-first century church is filled with numerous gifts: preaching, teaching, evangelism, administration, healing, speaking in tongues, and so on. Instead, our churches are lacking love. Where there is no love, there is no God because God is love. No matter what our churches do—build family life centers, support missions, administer soup kitchens—without love, our doing is in vain. One morning a guy tried to crank his car but it would not start. He performed several tests. Finally, he checked the water level in his battery and noticed it was low. After adding water to his battery, the car cranked up. Some of our churches need to check their spiritual batteries to see if we need to add more love. Then our pastors will be servants, people will be spiritual, and the world will be saved.

Truth 2—With love, our Christian character is exhibited (vv. 4–6).

In these verses, Paul listed the characteristics that would be exhibited by the Christian that possessed love. In verse 4, Paul elaborated on the meaning of love. One could say that these are the attributes, or characteristics, of love. Paul said that love is patient, which means forbearing, or long-tempered. This phrase would be parallel to the phrase *love is kind*. A deeper look into this latter phrase would reveal that love has an affect on the possessor; it makes that individual kind. Love also stops an individual from being jealous, a bragger, or arrogant. As Paul continued to disclose the connotations of love, he said that it is not rude or offensive. This means that when one exhibits love, it does not cause another individual to feel shameful or disgraced. Paul said that love is not self-seeking. Therefore, when one loves, that person does not expect to receive recompense, because love does not seek for itself.

Next, Paul said that love cannot be provoked. If the Corinthians expressed the love that is being preached, then it would have an effect on them so that they would not be aggravated or annoyed. Then Paul said that love does not keep a tally of wrongdoing. Again, if the Corinthians expressed the love that Paul is exhorting, they would be affected by this love and would not keep count of people's wrongs against them.

In verse 6, Paul continued to elaborate on the characteristics of love. He said that it does not rejoice in malevolence. So, the Corinthians were not supposed to delight in evil. Instead, they were to find joy or celebrate in the truth because Paul said that love rejoices in the truth. Paul said that if the Corinthians truly possessed *love*, they would admonish sin and exalt fidelity. When I envision the life of Jesus, I see the embodiment of the love that Paul was describing to the Corinthians. As we read the gospel narratives, we will notice that Jesus was patient and kind. He was not arrogant or a bragger. Jesus was not rude or offensive. He was neither self-seeking nor easily provoked. Jesus was not aggravated or annoyed. He did not keep count of wrongs and did not rejoice in evil.

When we possess love, we will be patient with one another and kind to each other. When we possess love, we will not be egotistical or boasters. When we possess love, we will not be impolite or unpleasant. When we possess love, we will not be selfish or easily aggravated. When we possess love, we will not keep a running tally of people's offenses toward us, nor will we celebrate in evil. If the church, which is the body of Christ, would follow the head (Christ), more love would be exhibited. More souls would be extracted from the grasp of Satan. And the Lord would be exalted.

Truth 3—With love, we have endurance (v. 7).

Paul said that love keeps all things confidential. Literally, this means "to put a roof on" or "to keep silent" about something. The members of the Corinthian church should be so exemplary in their love and confidentiality that others would believe that they could trust them with their innermost thoughts. Then Paul said that love entrusts or believes all. There is no doubt in love.. Next, Paul said that love hopes all things. In this instance, hope means to expect or await all. This could be a reference to the eschatological hope. Also, it could mean that it expects or awaits the best in all or everyone. I believe based on the context, hopes all things refers to our eschatological hope. Finally, love endures all. Paul was saying that if one possesses love, one is able to put up with all adversity and suffering. The Corinthians would need this love in order to be all that they needed to be as Christians. There is a hymn that says, "Yield not to temptation, for yielding is sin." Many times we are tempted, but with love, we can endure all manner of temptations. Even Jesus was tempted, but he did not yield to sin because he possessed this love. Our endurance is often put to the test.

Sometimes we are tempted to unveil someone's secret. But God knows our innermost sins and has not told anyone. We may be tempted to doubt the Word of God because of the supposed inaccuracy of the manuscripts. Our endurance may be put to the test while trying to hold on to a diminishing hope. I want to encourage you with Psalm 30:5 (ESV): "For his anger is but for a moment, and his favor is for a lifetime. Weeping may tarry for the night, but joy comes with the morning." It was the year 155 and Polycarp, a bishop of the early church, was on trial. With his answer determining his final fate, he decided not to worship the emperor. Polycarp said, "For eighty-six years I have served him, and he has done me no evil. How could I curse my king, who saved me?"[1] As Christians, we will be put on trial. The world will find us guilty. We shall be sentenced to death. It is then that we will be tempted to succumb to sin, but with the love of God, we can be like Polycarp and endure all temptation.

Conclusion

Do you have love? Do you believe it has a vital role in our Christian lives? In our text we noted that Paul's exposition on love signified its importance as a required characteristic in the life of the Corinthians. As Christians, we must realize that love is a necessary attribute in our lives, because love itself is necessary: God demonstrated it, Jesus commanded us to do it, the Holy Spirit reaches people through it, and Paul preached it. Therefore my desire is for you to possess it. Without love our spiritual gifts are not effective. With love our Christian character is exhibited. And with love we are able to endure all temptation.

---

1   Justo L. González, *The Story of Christianity*, vol. 1 (HarperOne, 2010), 54.

Invitation

Love: you can live with it, but you cannot live without it. If it was not for love, God's love, I would be spiritually dead. I thank God for his love because "God shows his love for us in that while we were still sinners, Christ died for us" (Rom. 5:8 ESV). Yes, we are sinners. The Bible reads, "All have sinned and fall short of God's glory" (Rom. 3:23 CEB). Do you know what the reward is for sin? Death! The Bible reads, "The wages of sin is death" (Rom. 6:23). But the good news is that because of God's love for us, we don't have to die. We can have eternal life: "For God so loved the world that he gave his one and only Son. Anyone who believes in [his Son Jesus Christ] will not die but have eternal life" (John 3:16 NIRV). Do you want to believe in Christ today? Do you want to learn more about Jesus Christ and how to have a relationship with him? Come and meet me at the altar, so we can talk about you and him.

QUESTION-ANSWER SERMON:
THE BEST GIFT EVER (JOHN 3:16–17)

Text

> For God so loved the world, that He gave His only begotten Son, that whoever believes in Him shall not perish, but have eternal life. For God did not send the Son into the world to judge the world, but that the world might be saved through Him. (John 3:16–17)

Introduction

What is the best gift you've ever received? PBS asked writers, musicians, and podcasters this same question.[2] Listen to a few of the responses PBS received:

- A filmmaker said the best gift ever was his daughter reciting Lincoln's Gettysburg Address on Christmas morning.
- A songwriter said the best gift ever was a reel-to-reel tape recorder given by his parents on Christmas day, 1969.
- A poet said the best ever gift was a baby ring she received from her mother when the poet was sixty-seven years old. She said her mother passed eight months later.
- An artist said the best gift ever was the inmates of San Quentin State Prison singing him happy birthday on his fiftieth birthday.
- A podcaster said the best gift he ever received was a 1976 Buick Regal his brother purchased for him when the podcaster was fifteen years old.
- One musician said the best gift ever was a bike that looked like a motorcycle, which his mom gave him on Christmas morning when he was nine years old.

---

2   Elizabeth Flock and Anne Azzi Davenport, "The Best Gift Ever, according to Thirteen Writers, Musicians and Podcasters," *PBS News Hour*, Dec. 21, 2017, https://www.pbs.org/newshour/arts/the-best-gift-ever-according-to-13-writers-musicians-and-podcasters.

- One author said, "My mother was born on Christmas. Obviously she is the best gift I ever received, in advance."
- Finally, one author said, "The word *gift* puts me in mind of my parents, who gave so much to their kids and asked for so little. If the marks of a great gift are that it recognizes who the recipient really is, and that it comes at a real cost to the giver, the best gifts my parents ever gave me were a dictionary and a typewriter. . . . And then, before I was 40, both of them died. It was a loss I'll never really get over. But it also liberated me to be who I needed to be, and to write what I needed to write, without fear of hurting them or incurring their moral judgment. They gave and gave, and then they died, and even their deaths were a kind of gift."

So what is the best gift you ever received? The best gift I ever received is a Bible. A Bible? Yes a Bible! Why the Bible? My mother bought me an *NIV Study Bible* about twenty years ago when I began preaching. The Bible is the best gift I ever received because it teaches me about the best gift ever. The Bible describes the best gift ever in John 3:16–17 (NASB 1995): "For God so loved the world, that He gave His only begotten Son, that whoever believes in Him shall not perish, but have eternal life. For God did not send the Son into the world to judge the world, but that the world might be saved through Him." After reading these verses, I have five questions about the best gift ever.

Sermon Points

Question 1: Who is the giver of this gift?

John 3:16 says, "For God . . .". God is the giver of the best gift ever. John called the giver of the gift *Theos*, which is part of the word for theology. Theology means the study of God. However, *Theos*, a common name for God in the New Testament, describes the person of God. *Theos* means God is "the one supreme supernatural being as creator and sustainer of the universe."[3] *Theos* means God is the one and only true God. For people who believe in the existence of multiple gods, *Theos* means God, the Christian God, is above all other gods. God is compassionate and gracious, slow to anger, and abounding in loving-kindness and truth.

I know we probably do not often go into this much detail with John 3:16, but when we understand the giver of the gift, then we will have a better appreciation and understanding of the gift. Because the gift was given by God, then it has to be the best gift ever. Because the gift was given by God, then it must be good and perfect. James 1:17 says, "Every good thing given and every perfect gift is from above, coming down from the Father of lights, with whom there is no variation or shifting shadow." God does not give us bad or broken gifts. God will not give me a good gift and give you a bad gift. God's gifts are good and perfect. So the best gift ever was given by God, and this gift is good and perfect. Now let's answer the second question.

Question 2: Who are the recipients of this gift?

The Scripture reads, "For God so loved the world . . .". John said the world is the recipient of God's gift. The "world" refers to people who are separated from God because of sin. Isaiah 59:2 (NASB 1995) reads, "But your iniquities have made a separation between you and your God, and your sins have hidden His face from you so that He does not hear." Before becoming Christians, all of us were a part of the world and its system because everyone was a sinner. Romans 3:23 says that all have sinned and come short of the glory of God. What is sin? Sin is disobeying God. When we sin, we miss the mark or fall short of God's standard. God's standard is holiness and righteousness. No matter how hard we try, we cannot meet God's expectations on our own.

---

3   Johannes P. Louw and Eugene Albert Nida, *Greek-English Lexicon of the New Testament: Based on Semantic Domains* (New York: United Bible Societies, 1996), 136.

Although we divide the world by classes, races, genders, and demographics, sin does not segregate. Everyone who is separated from God and misses the mark is a sinner. No matter how dark and depraved the world becomes, God still loves the world. The word for "love" here is *agape*. Sometimes we refer to this as unconditional love. This is true. However, *agape* also means a love that desires to see the greatest good for the object being loved. Even though the world disobeys God, he stills loves the world with an unshakeable kind of love. God's gift is for the world. This leads to our third question.

Question 3: What is the gift?

"For God so loved the world that he gave his one and only Son." The best gift ever is God's son, Jesus Christ. God gave the world his only begotten son. "Begotten" does not mean God birthed Jesus Christ. "Begotten" means unique, one of a kind, one and only. Some people consider the *Mona Lisa* the greatest portrait in the world. Why is the portrait so special? The *Mona Lisa* is special because of the artist and the portrait's availability. The artist was the famed Leonardo Da Vinci. The availability of the *Mona Lisa* is extremely limited. The *Mona Lisa* is an original and the only one of its kind. If the *Mona Lisa* was ever lost or destroyed, it could not be duplicated because the artist is deceased. So whoever possesses the *Mona Lisa* has something special. Jesus Christ is unique as well. When God gave the world his Son, it was not because he had several other sons lined up. Jesus is the only begotten Son of God. Jesus is original and one of a kind. As the Son of God, Jesus is not subordinate or less than God because Jesus is equal to God. Therefore no one is like Jesus. He is in a class all by himself. Jesus Christ is the best gift ever! Now we will answer the fourth question.

Question 4: What does the gift do?

"For God did not send his Son into the world to condemn the world, but to save the world through him." The best gift ever, Jesus

Christ, came into the world to save sinners. His first coming, or advent, was not to judge the world. His first coming was to save the world. In 1 Timothy 1:15 (NIV), the apostle Paul wrote, "Here is a trustworthy saying that deserves full acceptance: Christ Jesus came into the world to save sinners—of whom I am the worst." Jesus came to rescue or save sinners. In Colossians 1:13–14, the apostle Paul wrote, "For He rescued us from the domain of darkness, and transferred us to the kingdom of His beloved Son, in whom we have redemption, the forgiveness of sins." The world is drowning in sin, and Jesus is the lifeguard who came to save us. Jesus Christ coming to the world is a demonstration of how much God loved, or cherished, the world. Romans 5:8 reads, "But God demonstrates His own love toward us, in that while we were yet sinners, Christ died for us."

Since God knows all things, he knew some people would dishonor, deny, and ultimately murder Jesus Christ. Yes, Jesus was murdered. His death on the cross was the result of a false arrest, unjust trial, and a corrupt jury. However, the death of Jesus on the cross was necessary. Romans 6:23 reads, "For the wages of sin is death." Death is the result or payment we receive for our sins. However, Jesus died for the sins of the world. He died for your sins and mine. First Peter 3:18 (NASB 1995) reads, "For Christ also died for sins once for all, the just for the unjust, so that He might bring us to God, having been put to death in the flesh, but made alive in the spirit." Jesus Christ died so we could be forgiven of our sins and reconciled to God. So what does Jesus Christ do? He rescues sinners and reconciles them to God. Now we have made it to our fifth question.

Question 5: How do we receive this gift?

Jesus Christ is the best gift ever. As the only begotten son, he is the only edition. However, the salvation and reconciliation offered through Jesus Christ is available to all. We receive Jesus Christ and attain salvation and reconciliation. Let's look back at John 3:16: "For God so loved the world, that He gave His only begotten Son, that whoever believes in Him shall not perish, but have eternal life."

Receiving Jesus Christ is simple. All we have to do is believe in him. If you want to receive Jesus Christ, just believe in him. Many of us want to receive the benefits Jesus provides, salvation and reconciliation, without believing in Jesus. However, salvation and reconciliation are not available until you believe in him. John 1:11–12 (NASB 1995) reads, "He [Jesus] came to His own, and those who were His own did not receive Him. But as many as received Him, to them He gave the right to become children of God, even to those who believe in His name." When you believe in Jesus, you become a child of God and receive eternal or everlasting life. This means you will live forever with God. All of us will live forever. Our bodies will die, but our souls will continue to live. However, our souls will live forever in the presence of God or estranged from God. When we believe and receive Jesus Christ, we are rescued from sin and reconciled to God.

So what must we believe? We must believe that Jesus Christ is the Savior of the world and the Son of God. We must believe that he died for our sins and God raised him from the dead. We must believe that Jesus Christ is the way, the truth, and the life—the only way to God. So how do we believe in him? We put our faith in him. We place our hope and trust in Jesus Christ. We must stop depending on our works or good deeds to save us and restore our relationship with God. We must stop believing that we can save ourselves, thinking that when we stand before God at the final judgment, we will be received into heaven because we lived a good life according to worldly standards. If we want to spend eternity with God, we must believe in Jesus Christ, his death and resurrection.

Conclusion

"What is the best gift you've ever received?" According to PBS, people identified various gifts: songs, speeches, bicycles, and cars. In John 3:16–17, we see the best gift ever. God gave the best gift ever to the world. God gave the world his Son, Jesus Christ, to save the world and not condemn it. Whoever in the world receives and believes in Jesus Christ will not perish but have eternal life.

Invitation

I have one more question for you: What are you going to do with the best gift ever?

Several years ago, during my newlywed years, I was up late one night watching an infomercial. I forgot exactly what I saw on TV, but I ordered it. After I woke up a few hours later, I decided I did not want it anymore, so I called the company and asked how to cancel my order. The company said the order was already shipped but that when UPS came to deliver it, I could decline to receive the order. So UPS came, and I declined the order. The item was shipped back to the company and my money was refunded.

God sent us the best gift ever in Jesus Christ. This gift from God rescues us from deadly punishment of sin and reconciles us to God, the great Creator and Sustainer of the universe. So what are you going to do with the best gift ever? Will you receive him or reject him? And if you have already received him, will you give him to someone else?

THEN-NOW SERMON:
THE POWER OF PRAYER (PS. 107:6)

Text

Then they cried out to the LORD in their trouble;
He delivered them out of their distresses. (Ps. 107:6 NASB
1995)

Introduction

I believe the majority of Christians would agree that prayer is
powerful. Some may agree because of their personal experiences with
the power of prayer. They needed something miraculous to happen
in their lives. So they prayed and God answered in an overwhelming
and unexpected way. They became convinced regarding the power of
prayer because they had an Ephesians 3:20 experience. They prayed
and God gave them far more abundantly beyond all that they could
ask or think. It would be difficult to convince those Christians that
prayer is not powerful.

Although I believe the majority of Christians would agree that
prayer is powerful, I also think some Christians do not genuinely believe prayer is powerful, or they are indifferent about prayer altogether.
Why do I think this way? Because some Christians don't pray. Sure,
some may pray for their food because they have a superstition that
their stomachs will hurt if they don't pray for it. Or some think that
somehow choking on food is associated with not blessing it. Some
are so superstitious about this they will stop chewing and hold the
food in their mouths until they pray. Now forgetting to pray before
eating food does not mean a Christian does not believe in the power
of prayer; it's just an example of how many things we can do without
initiating prayer. And sometimes we initiate things without prayer
because we forget about the power of prayer.

Today I want to encourage you to pray in everything you do
because prayer is powerful. No matter how small or insignificant the
matter or issue may seem, you can cover it with the power of prayer.
Though I may share a few personal stories about the power of prayer,

we will open our Bible and look at God's book and see what it says about the power of prayer (read the text).

What does this text say about prayer? Prayer has the power to deliver us from our troubles.

Sermon Points: Then

The psalmist references how the power of prayer delivered people from trouble. In verses 4–5, the people wandered in the desert. They were homeless, hungry, and thirsty. Then they cried out to the Lord in their trouble; he delivered them out of their distress. In verses 10–12, some people lived in darkness and in the shadow of death. They scorned the counsel of the Most High God. Because of their rebellion and scorning, the Lord humbled them and subjected them to hard labor. They stumbled and fell, and there was no one to help them. So what did they do? The only thing they could do: they cried out to the Lord in their trouble, and he saved them out of their distress. In verses 18, they were starving and were close to the gates of death. Then they cried out to the Lord in their trouble, and he saved them out of their distress. In verses 26–27, they experienced the ups and downs of life. Their souls melted away. They reeled and staggered like a drunken man. They did not know what to do; they were at their wits' end. Then they cried out to the Lord in their trouble, and he brought them out of their distress. So when the people were in trouble, they cried out to the Lord and he delivered, saved, and brought them out of their distress. They prayed in their troubles and the power of prayer brought them out.

How did they pray? The Bible says they cried out—this means they shouted, called out with a sense of desperation, because of a difficult situation.

To whom did they pray? They cried out to the Lord. The word for "Lord" is *Yahweh* or *Jehovah*. Yahweh is the Creator and Sustainer of the universe. Yahweh is the King of the earth and sits on his throne in heaven, which makes the Lord transcendent, but Yahweh is also close to us, making him immanent. The people knew this truth. They knew that when they sinned, the Lord would seem distant, but when they drew near to him in prayer and repentance, he would be close to them. He would show up in the midst of their tragedy.

Why did they pray? They prayed in their trouble. This means they experienced affliction. They experienced some type of physical, mental, or socioeconomic adversity. Trouble is a stone or boulder too heavy to carry by yourself. Because of their troubles, they cried out to the Lord.

What happened after they prayed? The Lord delivered them out of their distress. He set them free. He broke their chains. He snatched them out of danger. He delivered them from their distress. In Hebrew, the word "distress" means psychological suffering. So whatever trouble they were facing, it affected their mindset. They needed the Lord to save their minds as well as their lives.

Sermon Points: Now

Do you need the power of prayer? Think about the following questions.

How do you pray when you are in trouble? Do you pray passively or passionately? When we are in trouble, we should pray with a sense of urgency. Pray like you want God to hear you. Pray like you want God to deliver you from your trouble. Pray like you feel the pain of your situation. Pray like you need a Savior. Pray like you want the chain broken. Pray with passion.

To whom do you pray? Every Christian does not pray to God first. I'm not implying that some Christians pray to another god, but I am saying we don't pray to God first. What do I mean that Christians don't pray to God first? Sometimes we call our family, friends, pastor, or group leader before we pray. I am suggesting that whomever we call or ask first is the person we are directing our prayers to. When you are in trouble, to whom do you pray? If you call mama first, then you are praying to mama. If you call daddy first, then you pray to daddy. I am not saying that we should not call other people, but many times we are disappointed because we call other people that we think can help us and *then* we call God. I encourage you to call God first; then he will tell you where to go for help. We should direct our pray to God first and foremost.

Why do you pray? My guess is you often pray when you are in trouble, you pray because you want to get out of trouble. You pray because you want freedom from your physical, mental, spiritual, social, or financial adversity. You pray because you want victory in your battle. You pray because no one can help you but God. However, don't wait until you get into trouble to pray. Sometimes if we pray before trouble, we can avoid trouble. Pray because you want to communicate and fellowship with God. Pray because you want to get closer to God. Pray because you want God to manifest his power in your life. Pray because you know that God is the only one that can remove the stone in your life. Mary asked the other women who would roll the stone away. God provided an angel to roll the stone away. You ask, Who will roll the stone away? God will roll the stone away.

What will happen after you pray? The Lord will hear you and respond. When the people prayed, cried out to God, he heard them and responded. If they were homeless, he gave them shelter. If they were in danger, he covered them with safety. If they were hungry, he provided with food. If they were wandering, he gave them direction. If they were at the gates of death, he put them on the path to life. When you pray, God will hear you and respond. How will you know the Lord has heard you? You will know the Lord has heard you because you will be delivered from your troubles. You will be delivered from your sickness. You will overcome your adversity. You will be victorious in your spiritual battles, secure in your finances, and free from the chains of insanity. However, God does not always answer in the way we expect. We may be delivered but trouble still surrounds us. Some of us are healed, yet are body is still weak. Some of us are victorious, but we are still under attack. Some of you almost lost your mind. You could not figure out why you were in trouble. You could not figure out how to get *out* of trouble. It almost drove you crazy, but God saved your mind. You know God has heard you because your stone is gone. The stone is the thing you couldn't move, the person you couldn't handle, the relationships you couldn't fix, the children you couldn't save, the job that stole your joy, the sickness you couldn't heal—that stone that was outside your door that you couldn't move—but now the stone is gone.

What if God does not answer my prayer? Sometimes we feel as if God does not respond to our prayers, but he always answers our prayers. He usually answers us in three ways—that is, yes, no, or not now. It is hard to discern between *no* or *not now* because the responses seem similar. However, it is possible to know if it is a no or not now. When God says "no," it is like he closes the door of opportunity and removes the knob of possibility. When God says "not now," he can leave the door open but not permit us to walk through it, or he can close the door and keep the key until we are ready to receive it. So a "not now" does not mean "never"; it just means "not at this moment." Although we all want to hear "yes," we should praise God for the "no"s and "not now"s because those answers have saved us from heartache and pain. So God hears us. Sometimes he does not respond they way we hope. God heard Jesus in Gethsemane when he God asked him to remove the cup of affliction. God say no. Paul asked God to remove his thorn, but God said no: "My grace is sufficient for you, for power is perfected in weakness" (2 Cor. 12:9).

Conclusion

So what can we take away from today's Scripture and sermon? First, prayer is powerful. Second, when we are in trouble, we should pray with a sense of urgency. Third, pray because you want to communicate and fellowship with God. Fourth, keep praying because the Lord will hear you and respond. Fifth, God answers our prayers with yes, no, or not now.

Invitation

Do you believe in the power of prayer? Jesus said, "If you ask Me anything in my name, I will do it" (John 14:14). What do you need today? Do you need love, joy, or peace? Ask Jesus! Do you need healing, help, or hope? Ask Jesus! Do you need a closer relationship with God? Ask Jesus! Do you need eternal life? Ask Jesus! Ask Jesus for whatever you need today!

KEY WORD SERMON:
RENEW OUR JOY (JAMES 1:2-8)

Text

Consider it all joy, my brothers and sisters, when you en-
counter various trials, knowing that the testing of your faith
produces endurance. And let endurance have its perfect
result, so that you may be perfect and complete, lacking
in nothing. But if any of you lacks wisdom, let him ask of
God, who gives to all generously and without reproach, and
it will be given to him. But he must ask in faith without any
doubting, for the one who doubts is like the surf of the sea,
driven and tossed by the wind. For that person ought not to
expect that he will receive anything from the Lord, being a
double-minded man, unstable in all his ways. (James 1:2–8)

Introduction

James was writing to the twelve tribes of Israel who were scattered
throughout the geographic regions east of Jerusalem known as Mesopo-
tamia, which is called the Middle East today. Like many of us, the Jews
James addressed were emotionally drained. The trials and tribulations
they were facing depleted their joy. So what did James say to them? He
told them to change their perspective regarding their trials. In verse 2
he wrote, "Consider it all joy, my brothers and sisters, when you en-
counter various trials." For those of us who need to renew our joy, we
have to change our perspective. What does it take for us to change our
perspective so we can renew our joy? I'm going to highlight five key
words that can help change our perspective on trials to renew our joy.

Sermon Points

1. Consider (v. 2)—viewpoint or opinion. We must change
   our viewpoint or opinion about trials.
2. Knowing (vv. 3–4)—to know, recognizing, be aware, or understand. We must know or understand that our trials have a
   purpose.

3. Ask (vv. 5–6)—pray. Prayer is an integral part of changing our perspective.
4. Wisdom (vv. 5)—act wisely. Apply your knowledge. We must ask for wisdom if we do not know how to apply this knowledge regarding trials.
5. Faith (vv. 6–8). We must ask for wisdom in faith.

Conclusion

Will you change your perspective? In order to understand trials, we must change our viewpoint about trials and realize trials have a purpose. Part of this realization comes through praying for wisdom. We must ask God for the ability to apply the wisdom we receive to the trials we face.

Invitation

Will you renew your joy? No Jesus! No joy! Know Jesus! Know joy! Come and talk with me and get to know Jesus today.

DEVOTIONAL SERMON:
A PRAYER FOR SPIRITUAL RENEWAL (PS. 51:10–12)

Text

> Create in me a clean heart, O God,
> And renew a steadfast spirit within me.
> Do not cast me away from Your presence
> And do not take Your Holy Spirit from me.
> Restore to me the joy of Your salvation
> And sustain me with a willing spirit. (Ps. 51:10–12 NASB 1995)

Introduction

After a tiresome 2020, and a turbulent kickoff for 2021, I believe we all need spiritual renewal. So how do we begin to renew our downtrodden spirits? It's simple! One word! *Prayer!* In this psalm, we notice that David needed spiritual renewal. So what did he do? He prayed! Prayer is our path to spiritual renewal. Prayer is an expression of our heartfelt desires to God. Prayer is what we need to revive our depressed and deadened spirits. Prayer is what the saints of old used to draw them near to God when they felt distant. Prayer is what we need for our spiritual renewal. So how do we pray for spiritual renewal? Our Scripture today, Psalm 51:10–12, is a prayer for spiritual renewal. David had committed adultery with Bathsheba and orchestrated the murder of her husband. So David really needed spiritual renewal. What did he say? These verses include three petitions for spiritual renewal.

Sermon Points

Petition 1: Lord, renew my spirit (v. 10).

Explanation
Create: shape, fashion
Clean: pure, free from sin and moral impurity

Renew: repair, restore
Steadfast: firm, upright

Illustration
Washing laundry

Application
We cannot renew our spirit.

Petition 2: Lord, let me remain in your presence (v. 11).

Explanation
Cast: throw away
Presence: face of God
Take your Holy Spirit from me

Illustration
David saw God take the Spirit from Saul.

Application
Social distance vs. spiritual distance

Petition 3: Lord, restore the joy of my salvation.

Explanation
Restore: bring back into original existence
Joy: gladness, happiness, pleasure
Salvation: deliverance from sin or trouble

Illustration
Restoring my mom's truck

Application
The restoration of joy begins with God, the origin of our joy.

Conclusion
Pray for renewal! Lord, renew my spirit! Lord, let me remain in your presence!
Lord, restore the joy of my salvation!

Invitation
Have you experienced the joy of salvation? Have you experienced salvation? Have you ever experienced the Savior, Jesus Christ? You can experience him and his salvation today!

ABOUT THE AUTHOR

Jesse L. Nelson (DMin, New Orleans Baptist Theological Seminary) is the senior pastor of Macedonia Missionary Baptist Church of Panama City, Florida, president of the Evangelical Homiletics Society, founding member of Pastors United of Bay County, and mayor of Lynn Haven, Florida. He is completing his PhD in Practical Theology (Homiletics) at Stellenbosch University. Dr. Nelson is an adjunct professor of pastoral ministry and has conducted preaching workshops in Haiti and the Dominican Republic. He has published articles and book reviews in the *Journal of the Evangelical Homiletics Society*, presented papers, and led a study group on African American Preaching at the Evangelical Homiletics Society Annual Scholars Conference. He is a contributing author to *The Handbook of Contemporary Preaching* and author of *We Survived Hurricane Michael: Stories and Sermons of God's Protection, Provision, and Power*. He is married to his high school sweetheart, Catesha. They have two children, Jacey and Carey, and a dog, Jumping Jack Sparrow.